The Black Dilemma
by John Herbers

Conflict and Compromise:
The Dynamics of American Foreign Policy
by Richard Halloran

Eastern Europe in the Soviet Shadow
by Harry Schwartz

Madman in a Lifeboat:
Issues of the Environmental Crisis
by Gladwin Hill

The USSR Today
by Harry A. Rositzke

# The New York Times

# SURVEY SERIES

---

## THEODORE M. BERNSTEIN
### GENERAL EDITOR

*The New York Times* SURVEY SERIES comprises books that deal comprehensively yet comprehensibly with subjects of wide interest, presenting the facts impartially and drawing conclusions honestly.

The series draws on the great information resources of *The New York Times* and on the talents, backgrounds and insights of specially qualified authors, mostly members of the *Times* staff.

The subjects range from the relatively particular problems of civilized life to the broadest conceivable problems concerning whether civilized life, or any kind of life, will continue to be possible on this planet.

The hope is that the books will be essentially informative, perhaps argumentative, but beyond that stimulative to useful, constructive thinking by the citizens who ultimately must share in civilization's decisions.

# Eastern Europe
# in the Soviet Shadow

# Eastern Europe in the Soviet Shadow

## HARRY SCHWARTZ

The John Day Company
An Intext Publisher
NEW YORK

Published in hardcover by
The John Day Company, 257 Park Avenue South, New York, N.Y. 10010


Published in softcover by
Intext Press, 257 Park Avenue South, New York, N.Y. 10010


Published on the same day in Canada by Longman Canada Limited.

Printed in the United States of America



**Library of Congress Cataloging in Publication Data**

Schwartz, Harry, 1919–
  Eastern Europe in the Soviet shadow.

  (New York times survey series)
  Bibliography: p.
  1. Europe, Eastern—Politics.  I. Title.
DR48.5.S384          327.4          72–2409
  ISBN:  0-381-98177-0  (hardcover)
              0-381-90003-7  (paperback)

To the Memory of My Father

# Contents

# Eastern Europe in the Soviet Shadow

# 1

# The Tinderbox
# of Europe

A PEASANT COTTAGE in the remote Yugoslav village of Kumrovec was the scene of a singular gathering on October 1, 1970. The cottage, the birthplace of President Tito in 1892, still contained the bed on which he was born. Sitting on the bed that day were Marshal Tito and his wife and their guests, President and Mrs. Nixon—all of them smiling, joking, and even clowning a bit for the benefit of a small army of photographers. The two statesmen were obviously making a strong effort to demonstrate their cordiality and friendship.

A year earlier President Richard Nixon had visited Rumania. The huge crowds that cheered him were a vivid contrast to the anti-Americanism he had encountered in other countries. Some observers suggested that the reception was perhaps the warmest an American President had received abroad for at least a decade. Yet Rumania, like Yugoslavia, is a Communist-ruled country. Then, in May 1972, President Nixon made formal state visits to the Soviet Union and Poland.

The closely spaced visits to Eastern Europe were unique

in the history of the American Presidency. Until comparatively recently Eastern Europe was little known to most
Americans, and even to many of their leaders. (That ignorance showed itself at the end of World War II, when American diplomatic dispatches dealing with Polish developments
contained misspelled names of major political leaders.) Nor
was the United States alone at fault among Western governments. In 1938 the British justified their sacrifice of Czechoslovakia to Hitler on the ground that it was a distant country
"of which we know little." The ignorance persisted even
though none could deny the central importance of Eastern
Europe—an area that, after all, was the tinderbox of Europe.
This area produced the sparks that ignited both World Wars
and it provided the immediate issues that gave birth to the
Cold War after 1945. President Nixon's visits testified to his
realization of Eastern Europe's importance. Why had earlier
generations of Western European and American political
leaders been so ill-informed about a region so vital to the
course of events? With respect to the United States at least,
the ignorance stemmed in part from the complexity of the
area—about which more below—and in part from a lack of
American scholarship on Eastern Europe.

There are more than a hundred million Eastern Europeans
in seven comparatively small countries: Albania (the small-
est, slightly larger in area than Maine), Bulgaria, Czechoslovakia, Hungary, Poland (the largest, about the size of New
Mexico), Rumania, and Yugoslavia. Each has its own traditions, culture, languages (several are multilingual), and problems.

As if that were not enough, they are plagued by internal
divergences. Czechoslovakia's fifteen million people consist

# The Tinderbox of Europe

mainly of a Czech majority and a Slovak minority, and much of Czechoslovakia's brief history has been determined by frictions between those two related but distinct peoples. The Yugoslav scene is even more complex since its population of twenty-one million consists of Serbs, Croats, Slovenes, Montenegrins, Bosnians, Macedonians, and Albanians, whose linguistic, cultural, and religious differences, and divergent political and economic aspirations cause deep tensions. Even Albania, with but two million inhabitants, is divided between the Ghegs, a mountain people with a tradition of fierce blood feuds, and the gentler Tosks, who live in the southern plains.

For a period after World War II, the West tended to regard all or most of Eastern Europe as a unified whole. The fact that the countries were ruled by Communist parties led many Westerners to think of them as Soviet satellites whose Moscow-imposed similarities blotted out their differences. The passage of time has demonstrated, however, that their unique national characteristics are not to be overlooked. No one can understand the situation in Eastern Europe or attempt to forecast its future without taking into account such factors as the fierce devotion of most of the thirty-two million Poles to Roman Catholicism, the democratic traditions of the Czechs, the resolve of the twenty million Rumanians to safeguard their Latin language and culture against the neighboring Slav peoples; the pride of the ten million Hungarians in their Magyar heritage and their former role as one of the two leading peoples of the Austro-Hungarian Empire (which died at the end of World War I), the continuing resentment of eight and a half million Bulgarians at being deprived of the large area of the Balkans which was ceded to them in 1878 and then quickly taken away.

Beneath the veneer of seeming Communist uniformity, the

5

Eastern European peoples were and are fiercely individualistic. They treasure their traditions and dream of the restoration of past glories. A brilliant flame of nationalism has long burned among them. Over the centuries each has fought hard to attain independence and to preserve it.

Through two thousand years this region has been the high road for innumerable invasions of Europe from Asia, as well as the battlefield on which rival empires have clashed. Roman, Hun, Mongol, Byzantine, Turkish, Austrian, German, Russian, and Italian armies have marched across Eastern Europe and ruled parts of it for months, years, or centuries. For most of the time since the American Revolution the great majority of its peoples have been the subjects of foreign powers, victims of alien oppression. On the eve of World War I the Polish nation was under German, Austro-Hungarian, and Russian rule; the Czechs were subject to Austria and the Slovaks to Hungary; the Albanians had just gained their freedom from Turkey. In 1914, too, there were many Rumanians, Bulgarians, and Serbs who still vividly remembered Turkish rule, which did not end until the last third of the nineteenth century.

It has been the misfortune of the Eastern European peoples that they have often been the victims of their larger neighbors' ambitions. But history shows that when they have had the power and the opportunity they, too, have exhibited imperialistic tendencies and have been just as ready to seize *their* neighbors' lands.

The ancient hostilities still simmer, even under the cloak of communist comradeship. The long animosity between the two northern Slav peoples—Poles and Czechs—helps explain why Poland gladly took part in the 1968 Soviet invasion of Czechoslovakia. Hungarians still mourn the loss of

6

rich Transylvania to Rumania and dream of reunification with their fellow Hungarians who live under Rumanian control. Yugoslavia, a federation of southern Slav peoples, is constantly alert for any move by Bulgaria to seize Yugoslav Macedonia, a region inhabited by people who the rulers in Sofia insist are really Bulgarians, not Macedonians. And the key to the complex foreign policy of Albania, which is allied with Communist China against the rest of the Communist bloc, has been fear of Yugoslav annexation. Simultaneously, some Albanian leaders dream of incorporating that area of Yugoslavia in which hundreds of thousands of ethnic Albanians are the dominant element.

Colonial rule over Eastern Europe for most of the last two hundred years has been the source of its pervasive and deep-rooted economic, technical, and educational backwardness. Through the centuries of foreign domination most of the people have been illiterate peasants, among whom feudal institutions survived much longer than they did in Western Europe. Not until after World War II did large-scale industrialization and the accompanying urbanization come to most of the area, which shared with Spain, Portugal, and southern Italy the unenviable distinction of being among the most underdeveloped parts of Europe before 1945.

Furthermore, the historic subjugation left divergent footprints. The greatest blight persisted in the southern Balkans, which had lived for centuries under harsh and degrading Ottoman Turkish rule in an atmosphere more suggestive of the Middle East than of Europe. Conditions were much better in parts of the Austro-Hungarian Empire, where there was more industry, more opportunity for education, and more scope for the development of a middle class of professionals and businessmen. The Czechs were perhaps the chief beneficiaries of the more advanced conditions under Austrian rule, while the Slovaks—dominated by feudal Hungarian masters—were a more backward, peasant people when the Austro-Hungarian realm collapsed.

The relatively advanced Croats and Slovenes of contemporary Yugoslavia demonstrate the benefits of having lived under Vienna's power, while other Yugoslav peoples have still not entirely shaken off the debilitating effects of the long era of Turkish misrule.

The stress on the relative backwardness of the Eastern European peoples, historically speaking, should not be misunderstood. There was and is much ability among them, and when conditions have been ripe they have made major contributions to culture and science.

Copernicus, a founder of modern astronomy, was a Pole, as were the composer Frédéric Chopin and Marie Curie, the discoverer of radium. The Czechs gave the world one of the pioneers of the Protestant Reformation, the martyred Jan Hus, as well as the great educational innovator Comenius. In more recent times the Czechs have produced such world-famous composers as Smetana and Dvorak. The nuclear age is in part the product of a group of Hungarians transplanted to the United States in the 1930's—men such as Leo Szilard, Edward Teller, Eugene Wigner, and John von Neumann. Modern electrical technology owes much to the contributions of Yugoslavs Michael Pupin and Nikola Tesla; a fundamental geological feature, the so-called Mohorovicic Discontinuity, is named after its Yugoslav discoverer. As long ago as the fifteenth century the Albanians had a national leader, Scanderbeg, whose heroic exploits while leading his people's resistance to the Turks won him world fame.

Indirectly, the United States has greatly benefited from the backwardness, poverty, and political oppression that were so long the lot of most Eastern Europeans. In the nineteenth and early twentieth centuries millions of Poles, Czechs, Slovaks, Hungarians, Rumanians, Croats, Slovenes, Serbs, Bulgarians, and Albanians migrated westward, impelled by the quest for economic improvement and the desire for freedom. The immigrants provided much of the manpower required by the steel mills, manufacturing plants, railroads, and other enterprises of industrial America. Their children learned English and moved up the economic, political, and social ladder. Senator Edmund S. Muskie of Maine, the son of a Polish immigrant, was the Democratic candidate for Vice President of the United States in 1968, and there were descendants of Eastern European immigrants among the astronauts who blazed the United States trail to the moon in the 1960's.

When World War I began enough Eastern Europeans had become United States citizens and voters to form a significant political force as well as a source of aid to their compatriots struggling for independence back home. Their political pressure helped buttress President Woodrow Wilson's insistence on self-determination for the peoples freed after the collapse of Germany, Austria-Hungary, Russia, and Turkey in 1917 and 1918. (Americans whose parents or grandparents came from Eastern Europe have continued to play an active political role. Their bitter hostility to Moscow's domination helped to stiffen United States resistance to Soviet imperialism in Eastern Europe after 1945.)

With the disintegration of empires, a temporary power vacuum developed in Eastern Europe after World War I, and its peoples were quick to take advantage of the situation to establish national states that, with some major boundary changes, have survived. In part, their size and population were determined by Wilson and his British and French colleagues, who dictated the peace to the defeated powers at Versailles. To Wilson, the important consideration was satisfaction of the national aspirations of the peoples of Eastern Europe—an attitude that spelled the reduction of Austria and Hungary to small, weak states. But in the confusion of the postwar period, much depended also upon the military power each new state could muster against its neighbors.

At that time the creator of reborn Poland, Marshal Jozef Pilsudski, dreamed of re-establishing the golden age of the Jagiellonian Empire (1386–1572) and sought to conquer Lithuania and the Russian Ukraine. He captured Kiev for a time, but a counterattack carried the Red Army almost to the gates of Warsaw before a compromise was reached.

Rumania and other neighbors of defeated Hungary seized as much Hungarian territory as they could, taking full advantage of the short-lived Hungarian Communist regime under Bela Kun. The fighting and political maneuvering were finally ended in June 1920, when Hungary was forced to sign the Treaty of Trianon, which ceded to others more than half of Hungary's prewar area and population. Many Hungarians still regard the treaty as a terrible disaster and remain bitter toward Czechoslovakia, Yugoslavia, and Rumania. Czechoslovakia and Yugoslavia, incidentally, were the political progeny of World War I. Czechoslovakia was created by Thomas G. Masaryk (he established its basis at a meeting in Pittsburgh and acquired an American wife while he was in the United States) as a union of Czechs and Slovaks. Yugoslavia emerged as a federation of southern Slavs built around the Serbian kingdom.

Wilson and his supporters envisioned a new era of national

independence, freedom, and prosperity for Eastern Europe. The reality was quite different in most of the area during the period between the two wars. Except in Czechoslovakia, democracy proved to be a weak force and gave way to dictatorships, military or royal, in the six other countries. There were persistent economic hardships. Far from being secure in their new independence, all the states found their existence threatened in the 1930's and several were subjugated by Nazi Germany's military and economic power even before World War II. As early as 1940, then, it was evident that the Wilsonian experiment in self-determination and national independence was a failure.

What went wrong? Among the many contributory factors were mistakes by the leaders, but much more important were the pressures flowing from military, economic, and political developments elsewhere.

It is amazing in retrospect that anyone should have expected democracy to flourish in the region after World War I. Few of the peoples had had experience with democratic institutions. There were bitter internal divisions based on class or nationality, or both.

Czechs and Slovaks soon discovered that they mistrusted one another, the Czechs looking on the Slovaks as ignorant hillbillies, the Slovaks viewing the Czechs as arrogant oppressors attempting to deny Slovakia its just due. In Yugoslavia the Serbs sought to dominate the new state under a centralized government while the Croats and other minorities fought for more local power. In Poland conflict between economic groups was superimposed upon a policy of discrimination that angered Ukrainians, Jews, and the other minorities that were significant segments of the population.

In the resulting political maelstroms, Marshal Pilsudski

11

seized power in a Polish *coup d'état* in 1926. King Alexander established a Yugoslav dictatorship early in 1929. King Boris of Bulgaria suppressed political parties and closed their newspapers in 1934. Hungary had an authoritarian regime under the regent, Admiral Nicholas Horthy, through most of the period. There were similar undemocratic patterns in Rumania under King Carol in the 1930's and in Albania under King Zog. Only in Czechoslovakia, under the leadership of Masaryk and Eduard Benes, did democracy stand firm.

Vitally important, too, was the fact that the territorial and political changes after World War I disrupted old economic channels and trade connections. All the countries were poor and underdeveloped. They all needed capital investment to build industry, increase production, and provide jobs, but there was little domestic capital, and foreign sources withered as the Great Depression caused major bank failures in Germany and Austria.

The depression struck savagely throughout Eastern Europe, drying up essential foreign markets, increasing unemployment, impoverishing the peasantry and making a good part of the area easy prey to the machinations of Hitler's financial and economic genius, Hjalmar Schacht. With unemployment and misery so widespread, right-wing demagogues could readily whip up anti-Semitism, making the Jews in several of the countries the scapegoats for economic difficulties.

Finally, until the larger states were in a position to try to fill the gulf left by World War I, the Eastern Europeans were particularly threatened, as we have seen, by their mutual antagonisms and territorial disputes. Hungary never hid its desire for revenge, building a giant statue in Budapest to symbolize its yearning for the territories seized by its neighbors. The territories were depicted on a floral map in the capital's main park; the national attitude toward acceptance of the losses was summed up in the motto: *Nem, nem, soha!* (No, no, never!). Bulgaria, in turn, coveted Yugoslav Macedonia, and Albania wanted Yugoslav Kossovo.

The power vacuum collapsed in the 1930's as Germany under Hitler, the Soviet Union under Stalin, and Italy under Mussolini gained military power. The Eastern European nations found themselves in a vise, imperiled on all sides by totalitarian systems that could establish fifth columns to undermine them. Hitler used German minorities, notably in the Sudetenland of Czechoslovakia; Mussolini encouraged native fascist groups; Stalin employed Communist parties, many of them illegal and working under extremely difficult underground conditions.

The pressure of the competing totalitarian states helped to reinforce the trend toward dictatorship in Eastern Europe, but dictatorship by itself could not strengthen a country enough to prevent invasion.

Ideally the Eastern European states should have presented a solid military and political front against potential aggressors, but such unity was precluded by their discords and mutual jealousies. The major alliance that was forged—the so-called Little Entente uniting Czechoslovakia, Rumania, and Yugoslavia—had mutual defense against Hungarian territorial claims as a major objective. In 1934 Yugoslavia and Rumania allied themselves with Greece and Turkey in a Balkan Pact, among whose purposes was mutual defense against the territorial claims of Bulgaria and Albania. Czechoslovakia sought to buttress its security against rising German power by entering into an alliance both with France (which played an active role in supporting the Little Entente) and with the Soviet Union.

Poland, primarily fearful of the Soviet Union, sought to remain on good terms with France and Germany. But the "dictatorship of colonels" that assumed power after Pilsudski's death in 1935 cast covetous eyes on the Silesian area of Teschen in Czechoslovakia, and looked forward to benefiting from what the Poles regarded as Czechoslovakia's inevitable destruction. They took it for granted that there would be a "holy war" between Nazi Germany and Communist Russia and dreamed of a neutral "third Europe" of eastern states that could stand aloof from the fray. The Polish Foreign Minister, Josef Beck, expected to dominate this third Europe, which he proposed to base on a Polish-Hungarian axis—after he had helped Hungary regain Slovakia—and to include Rumania and Yugoslavia. In the end those illusions helped destroy Poland.

Hitler had his own plans and, no less important, he had the military power to realize his ambitions. He saw a Europe ruled by the German superman, a continent in which the Aryans his fantasy discerned in Germany would be served by the enslaved "inferior" peoples of Eastern Europe. He might have been stopped earlier if the intended objects of his aggression had combined against him, but that was not to be. Instead the key European countries retreated into isolationism and, more shamefully, demonstrated that they were ready to betray their friends and neighbors in the persistent hope that just one more act of appeasement would satisfy Hitler's appetite.

There was a strong peace movement in the democracies, and many people believed that wars were caused by the machinations of the "merchants of death"—today's "military-industrial complex." Unwilling to fight to protect others, the peoples of Europe let Hitler's power grow until finally most of them had to fight to defend themselves in the most terrible war in history. Hitler was helped, too, by the general fear of Soviet Communism and the resulting reluctance of France and Britain—partly based on an underestimation of Soviet military potential—to cooperate with Stalin in stopping the Nazis.

It took Hitler only about a year and a half to undermine the structure formed in Eastern Europe after World War I. Then his effort to conquer the region precipitated World War II. All went well at first as he exerted pressure by charging Czechoslovakia with discrimination against the more than three million Sudeten Germans. President Benes frantically sought to build up his country's defenses while making concessions in the Sudetenland. The Sudeten party, led by Konrad Henlein, became in effect the Czechoslovak branch of the Nazi party and won the support of two-thirds of the Sudeten Germans.

When Hitler seized Austria on March 12, 1938, without serious opposition, the fate of Czechoslovakia became obvious, especially since German military, political, and propaganda preparations for an attack were unmistakable. The main question was whether Czechoslovakia's allies, France and the Soviet Union, would come to its aid.

The Czechoslovaks were betrayed, as it turned out, but the action was hailed in many quarters as an assurance of "peace in our time." The chief betrayers were Prime Minister Neville Chamberlain of Britain and the French Premier, Édouard Daladier. Meeting with Hitler and Mussolini in Munich at the end of September 1938, the British and French leaders signed an agreement forcing Czechoslovakia to cede to Ger-

15

many within ten days' time all areas that had had German majorities in 1910. No one bothered to ask the opinion of the Czechoslovaks who, faced with the combined power of Britain, France, Germany, and Italy, had no choice. Poland, grasping the opportunity, demanded the Teschen area from Czechoslovakia; Hungary called for a slice of Slovakia. The naïve hopes that appeasement had satisfied Hitler or assured peace were soon dispelled. In mid-March of 1939 he seized the Czech regions and turned Slovakia into a puppet "independent" state.

After Hitler had demonstrated to Mussolini how easy and safe it was to conquer helpless Eastern European states, Italian forces the next month invaded Albania and, after a short struggle, subdued it. King Victor Emanuel of Italy added King of Albania to his name and the territory became an Italian province.

By that time Britain and France had realized Hitler could not be appeased, and frantically began to prepare for war. Hoping to save something in Eastern Europe, they guaranteed the independence and territorial integrity of Poland and Rumania and, reluctantly, began negotiating for an alliance with the Soviet Union. Hitler, who had marked Poland as his next victim, carried on secret discussions with Stalin aimed at neutralizing the Russians while German troops prepared to march into Poland. Stalin, already angered by the obvious reluctance of the British and French to join him, made sweeping demands during the negotiations with the Western powers, insisting in particular that Poland admit Soviet troops. Faced with a choice of alliances, the Soviet dictator selected Nazi Germany in preference to the West.

A profound shock was felt around the world with the announcement of the Hitler-Stalin Pact of August 1939.

16

Nominally a nonaggression treaty, it actually was a political alliance which enabled Hitler to invade Poland. A secret protocol provided that Germany and the Soviet Union would divide Poland and the Baltic states—Estonia, Latvia, and Lithuania—between them. In addition, Stalin won what amounted to Hitler's agreement to the seizure of Bessarabia from Rumania. Even in the world of diplomacy that was an extraordinarily cynical deal between two countries and two ideologies that had proclaimed themselves bitter enemies.

The German invasion of Poland in September began World War II because, this time, Britain and France honored their pledge to an Eastern European country by moving against Germany, but they were far away and of little help as Nazi tanks and infantry knifed their way eastward toward Warsaw. Two weeks after the German invasion Soviet troops also entered Poland, and the struggle was soon over. Poland disappeared from the map as its territory and people were shared between Stalin and Hitler.

Rumania was the next to be dismembered. On June 26, 1940, the Soviet Foreign Minister, Vyacheslav M. Molotov, issued a demand that the Rumanians hand over Bessarabia and northern Bukovina. German support of Moscow allowed Rumania no alternative. A few weeks later it had to cede more territory to allies of the Germans: southern Dobruja to Bulgaria and northern Transylvania to Hungary. Rumania, with a third of its territory and population gone, was reduced to the status of a German satellite.

Now that the map of the Balkans had been redrawn, new friction appeared in the German-Soviet relationship. Hitler was alarmed by signs that Moscow wanted to annex Bulgaria and what remained of Rumania. Stalin was displeased by

17

evidence that the Germans were helping the Rumanians increase their ability to resist further Soviet pressure. He was also angered when the Bulgarians admitted German troops in March 1941. The tensions helped push Hitler toward his fateful decision to invade the Soviet Union.

The attack would have come earlier than June 22, 1941—and might have been more successful—if Yugoslavia had not temporarily diverted Hitler's attention. Under German and Italian pressure, the Belgrade government signed a treaty in March 1941, making itself an ally, i.e., a satellite, of Berlin and Rome. Angered by the treaty, the Yugoslav people were delighted when a group of air force officers staged a *coup d' état* and installed an anti-German regime. Overnight the national slogan became: "Better war than the treaty, better death than slavery." Infuriated, Hitler replied with all his power: Belgrade was bombed repeatedly and the Germans invaded from Bulgaria, Hungary, and Rumania. Hungarian and Italian troops also participated in the onslaught, which destroyed the Yugoslav Army within a few weeks.

By early May 1941 Hitler was the master of Eastern Europe, but his projected invasion of the Soviet Union had been delayed by what proved to be a crucial four weeks.

Yugoslavia paid for its brave resistance by being broken up. Germany took most of Slovenia. The rest went to Italy, which also seized the Dalmatian coast and Montenegro. Hungary, Bulgaria, and Italian-occupied Albania shared in the booty. An independent Croatian state was created under Ante Pavelich, leader of the nationalist, terrorist Ustashi; a Serbian state was also established, but it had even less "independence" than the Croatian one.

In short, Hitler emerged as the chief beneficiary of the Eastern Europe designed by Woodrow Wilson and the nationalist forces he supported. The Führer, exemplifying the classic tactic of dividing and conquering, gobbled up the Eastern Europeans because their countries were too small and disunited to forge an effective resistance. He demonstrated that a powerful and unscrupulous government could easily dominate Eastern Europe. The lesson was not lost on Stalin, who showed his own virtuosity a few years later in combining power and diplomacy to make himself the master of the region.

# 2

# Eastern Europe Under Stalin

A SOVIET FILM glorifying the capture of Berlin by the Red Army was being shown in a theater in the Soviet sector of that city in July 1945. The high point was a scene in which several Soviet soldiers risked their lives to save a German civilian caught in cross fire. When the lights went on Germans in the audience crowded around some Americans to denounce the film. The conquering Russians had not been gallant liberators, the Berliners insisted angrily, but plunderers and rapists.

At the time I was inclined to dismiss the episode as unimportant, but I came to understand that throughout Eastern Europe millions of people looked on Soviet soldiers with loathing because of their cruel and rapacious behavior after their triumph.

With the defeat of the Nazis, the Soviet Union became the military master of Eastern Europe. What was to become of the area now? Would its peoples determine their own destinies or would yet another era of colonial rule be imposed upon them? Those were the questions that underlay the discussions between Roosevelt, Churchill, and Stalin at the Yalta Conference and subsequent meetings.

Defeated Germany, the victorious allies had agreed, would be governed as a whole through mechanisms to be set up by the United States, the Soviet Union, Britain, and France working together. Czechoslovakia, Poland, and Yugoslavia, which had been conquered by Hitler, and Albania, which had fallen to Mussolini, were presumably in a more favorable position than Hungary, Rumania, and Bulgaria, all Hitler's allies. Reparations could be demanded of the defeated nations, but hardly, it would appear, from those countries that had been overrun and victimized by the Nazis. As for government, it seemed appropriate that power would be assumed in the defeated Eastern European countries by allied control commissions in which the Russians would have the decisive voice.

If the Western Allies and the Soviet Union had been able to agree on the future of Eastern Europe, the world since 1945 might have become a very different place. The bitter conflict over that area initiated the Cold War, with its great costs and great dangers.

Disputes over the responsibility for the Cold War persist, but to Westerners who lived through its development the reality seemed plain enough. First the Russians looted Eastern Europe of much of its machinery and other wealth and shipped it back to help rebuild Soviet areas devastated by the war. Then, using their military power, they helped Communists establish dictatorships in all seven countries, though the Communists had little popular support.

In the West there were growing fears that the same fate might be in store for Western Europe and beyond if Stalin were not resisted. However, the United States government made a last-ditch effort to avoid the division of Europe into hostile areas by offering massive economic aid—the Marshall Plan—to all war-devastated countries. Stalin rejected it and ordered the Eastern European countries to follow suit, although several wanted to accept American help.

Early in 1949 Stalin advanced his alternative to the Marshall Plan—the Council for Mutual Economic Assistance, known as Comecon, which was primarily a means of integrating the Eastern European economies with that of the Soviet Union rather than a mechanism for extending aid. Comecon did not become of significant importance until much later, but Stalin's pressure on Eastern Europe to reject the Marshall Plan joined with the emotional and dramatic circumstances that surrounded the Communist *coup d'état* in Czechoslovakia in February 1948, to put the final seal on the division of Europe.

In ceremonial declarations during World War II, Stalin, Roosevelt, and Churchill pledged themselves to the formation of democratic governments with full rights of self-determination in the countries freed from Nazi rule. When it came to considering precise arrangements, Churchill and Stalin were much concerned with their interests in the area but, except for the case of Poland, Roosevelt was less involved because he discerned no major American interests there.

It is not surprising, then, that a major policy decision on the region's future was concluded in a private conversation between Churchill and Stalin in the Kremlin in October 1944. The British leader proposed that the Soviet Union enjoy 90 per cent "predominance" in Rumania, 75 per cent in Bulgaria, and 50 per cent in Yugoslavia and Hungary, the remaining influence to be shared by the United States and

Britain. In Greece, on the other hand, Britain and the United States would have 90 per cent and the Soviet Union 10 per cent. Stalin approved the suggestion, which Churchill had penciled on a piece of paper.

Apparently embarrassed by the scope of the deal, Churchill told Stalin: "Might it not be thought rather cynical if it seemed we had disposed of these issues so fateful to millions of people in such an offhand manner? Let us burn the paper." Stalin's reply was, "No, you keep it."

Churchill insisted in his memoirs that the agreement dealt only with immediate wartime plans and that "all larger arrangements were reserved on both sides for what we then hoped would be a peace table when the war was won." In any case, the percentages had little real meaning; the reality even before Germany's surrender was that in all the countries occupied by the Red Army the Soviet Union exercised virtually 100 per cent control.

There were years of wrangling as the United States and Britain sought a hand in shaping Poland's future. During World War II a Polish government in exile in London had had American, British and—for a time—Soviet diplomatic recognition and support. Moscow helped the London Poles recruit an army from Polish refugees and prisoners of war in Soviet territory. The London Poles also benefited from President Roosevelt's sensitivity to the large American population of Polish origin, which demanded restoration of a free and independent Poland. Moreover, the Polish government in exile controlled a large underground, which was an effective force until the bloody Warsaw uprising against the Nazi occupiers in 1944.

The London Poles, despite their assets, were frustrated in

their hope of taking power in liberated Poland. It was Stalin's army that drove out the Germans, and by that time he regarded the London Poles as his enemies. Not only were they representatives of "bourgeois" parties but they had dared raise the possibility that Soviet troops might have slaughtered the hundreds of Polish officers whose bodies were discovered in the Katyn Forest.

Stalin installed the so-called Lublin government, dominated by Communists and their sympathizers who had returned with the Red Army after having spent the war years in the Soviet Union. Under heavy pressure from the Western powers, he did agree to admit some London Poles into the government, but within two or three years the most important ones had been driven out of political life. Stalin was aided in this by the fact that much of the anti-Communist underground had been exterminated in the Warsaw uprising —during which the Red Army sat across the river doing nothing.

No less important than the new government Stalin gave Poland were the new boundaries he imposed. Keeping the areas of eastern Poland he had annexed in 1939 in agreement with Hitler, he compensated the Poles by turning over 39,000 square miles of eastern Germany bounded on the west by the Oder and Neisse rivers, which are less than a hundred miles from Berlin.

The Polish government moved quickly to evict the German inhabitants and replace them with Poles. Inevitably, the territorial realignment made all Poles, regardless of politics, fear a resurgent Germany. Stalin undoubtedly foresaw that their desire to retain the Oder-Neisse line as their western border would force the Poles to look to the Soviet Union for aid.

Immediately to the west of the new Poland is the German Democratic Republic, an area generally known as East Germany and formerly as the Soviet Zone of Germany. Geographically it was Central Germany before World War II and does not belong to Eastern Europe as defined here, although it, too, is a Communist-ruled state, and we shall deal with it only briefly as necessary. Its emergence was the result of the collapse of the original plans for joint four-power rule over all Germany. As the East-West split deepened after 1945, the Soviet Union assumed unilateral political control over the segment its troops occupied. Later it authorized the formation there of a "sovereign state," the German Democratic Republic, under the dictatorship of the veteran German Communist leader, Walter Ulbricht. Much of European politics since World War II has revolved around Moscow's effort to have the Communist-ruled portion of Germany universally recognized as a legitimate state entitled to legal parity with West Germany.

From the end of World War II until Stalin's death in 1953, Soviet policy in East Germany was dominated by the desire to milk the area of as many resources as possible to aid reconstruction at home. The burden of the heavy reparations payments, added to the cost of supporting the large Soviet armies in East Germany, kept economic conditions extremely depressed. West Berlin, the small Western-ruled enclave in East Germany, provided a useful window from which to see the growing economic contrast. In the mid-1950's anyone who took the short subway ride from West to East Berlin moved between two worlds, from the prosperity and hope of West Berlin to the gray misery of the East. Not only was East Germany poor in those days, but it was subject, as it still is, to the rigors of a secret police-based

25

totalitarianism matching that of Stalinist Russia. Little wonder that in the 1950's, when the way was still open, thousands of East Germans fled to the West through West Berlin.

For two reasons Czechoslovakia was a special case among Eastern European countries at the end of World War II. First, the leaders of the Czechoslovak government-in-exile were willing to cooperate with the Czechoslovak Communist party, which had been an important political group before Hitler's takeover. Second, Eduard Benes, Thomas Masaryk's successor, understood the facts of power in Eastern Europe and was far more willing to consider the wishes of the Soviet Union than were the Polish exiles. Benes gave quick consent when Moscow demanded that he cede the Carpatho-Ukraine, the extreme eastern tip of Czechoslovakia, to the Soviet Union, though it has never been part of Russia. Benes dreamed in vain of turning Czechoslovakia into a bridge between East and West, seeking to combine Socialism and democracy at home, while trying to help keep the victorious World War II allies united.

Early in 1948 it looked for a time as if pending free elections might eliminate the Communists from the government. The elections were not held. Instead, masses of armed Communist workers were mobilized in Prague to force the non-Communist members of the coalition to resign. Broken by the brutal seizure of power, Benes died shortly afterward. The Foreign Minister, Jan Masaryk, son of Thomas Masaryk and a non-Communist, also died a few days after the coup, falling from his window in an incident that was officially labeled suicide although many suspected murder.

The course of events in Bulgaria, Hungary, and Rumania from 1945 to 1948 was roughly parallel to developments in

26

Poland and Czechoslovakia, although there were differences in detail and timing, of course. Initially, coalition governments with Communist and non-Communist elements were established. Typically, a new regime would carry out land reforms, distributing large estates among poor peasants. It would nationalize the property of those who had collaborated with the Germans and punish those guilty of war crimes. Relative freedom of speech and the press was allowed and there was genuine competition for political influence and power. In Hungary, in November 1945, there was even a free election, held under the supervision of the Red Army, in which the Communist party received only 17 per cent of the votes; the non-Communist Smallholders party, representing the peasant majority, won 57 per cent.

From the outset, nevertheless, it was plain that Communists occupied a special position of power and privilege. Party members and sympathizers were usually represented in proportions far exceeding their popular support. Moreover, the Communists and their fellow travelers usually received the ministerial posts controlling the armed forces and the secret police, putting them in vital positions for the future. Communists usually directed the land-reform programs so that the party could gain popularity among the peasant majorities. And after the 1945 Hungarian election, the Communists were shielded from having to seek votes in competition with more popular parties; instead the voters were asked to endorse coalitions including the Communists.

Those coalitions in which non-Communists exercised genuine power and influence did not last long. They were destroyed by what one Communist leader called "salami tactics"—cutting off a little bit at a time. Opposition leaders were thrown in jail, beaten in the streets, or threatened with

27

death. Hecklers broke up non-Communist meetings. The increasingly Communist-controlled press denounced non-Communist leaders as imperialist spies or Nazi agents.

As more and more non-Communists were ousted or jailed, those who remained became increasingly fearful. Many fled abroad, others simply capitulated and did as they were told and still others left political life. The result was a monopoly of power, although the Communists sought to present a façade of democracy by permitting some puppet "non-Communist" parties to survive and have representation.

Except for Czechoslovakia, the Eastern European countries had had at most only a few thousand Communist party members when the Red Army arrived. To recruit members quickly, the parties simply opened their membership lists to ambitious careerists, promising a share in the fruits of power for those who would help seize it (even former fascists were accepted if they were willing to do as they were told). Many of the Communist leaders who suddenly appeared in high posts were virtually unknown refugees who had returned from the Soviet Union. In Poland there were so few capable native Communists that many important positions were given to Soviet citizens of Polish ancestry.

The new rulers of Eastern Europe—Boleslaw Bierut and Jakob Berman in Poland, Klement Gottwald and Rudolf Slansky in Czechoslovakia, Matyas Rakosi in Hungary, Ana Pauker in Rumania, and George Dimitrov in Bulgaria— knew well that they owed their power to Soviet influence. Most of them needed little urging to obey Stalin's dictates.

After the Communists, ignoring repeated Western protests against the betrayal of Soviet commitments, had entrenched themselves in Eastern Europe, there was pressure on all the countries—except Yugoslavia, which had broken the traces—to make themselves small-scale models of the Soviet Union. They became Communist dictatorships whose control was enforced by a secret police organized and operated on the pattern of the Soviet secret police. The entire press was turned into a propaganda chorus on the model of *Pravda* and *Izvestia.*

Political opponents who had not succeeded in fleeing were jailed and many thousands of anti-Communists were put to slave labor. Stalin was glorified as the wisest, kindest, and best of men whose every word was law for lesser mortals. Intensive campaigns of Russification got under way: the study of Russian was required in schools, Russian movies dominated the theaters, and translations of Soviet works flooded the bookstores.

On the economic side, virtually all industry, transport, banking, and foreign trade were nationalized, and intensive campaigns began in the rural areas to collectivize agriculture on Soviet lines. The free market was essentially wiped out and centralized economic planning was introduced. Intensive programs of industrialization were undertaken, giving priority to heavy industry.

In 1950, when the Korean War started, the emphasis shifted to the production of weapons for the war with the United States which Stalin feared might be imminent. With free speech and press abolished and with secret police agents vigilant everywhere to catch those so incautious as to voice even a subversive joke, a miasma of fear hung over Eastern Europe. But underneath the enforced public unanimity and approval, dangerous tensions and enormous tides of dissatisfaction were building up.

The frantic pace of industrialization required huge sacrifices and lower living standards. As millions were moved from the farms to the cities to man new factories and construction sites, housing became a nightmare and the Soviet style of one room to a family became usual throughout Eastern Europe.

Adding to the workers' discontent was the discovery that their unions existed to make them work harder, not to defend their interests. Farmers coerced into collectives felt betrayed; only a few years earlier they had regarded land reform as a vast improvement over the prewar situation. Intellectuals were bitterly indignant over the tight censorship and the demand that literature and art serve propaganda purposes.

Almost everywhere in nationalistic Eastern Europe, the subservience to Moscow and the compulsory glorification of the Russian language and Soviet culture were widely resented. Among Eastern Europeans in general there was anger at Communist efforts to eradicate religious belief.

The postwar years may have been an ordeal, but there were also positive developments. Throughout the region education facilities, from kindergarten to college and beyond, were rapidly expanded. The goal was the development of a literate labor force and of large numbers of skilled workers, engineers, chemists, and other specialists required for industrialization. Medical services were also increased; an effective labor force, the new rulers realized, had to be a healthy labor force. Efforts were made to lessen the national hatreds and animosities that had roiled relationships in the area for so long. Poles and Czechs, Czechs and Slovaks, Rumanians and Hungarians, all were told to forget old antagonisms and to work together for the Communist utopia. Anti-Semitism, so strong and poisonous a force in the past, was also discouraged, although only a tiny fraction of the prewar Jewish population had survived the Nazi slaughter. But anti-Semitism continued to be an important underground force, fostered by the fact that a few hundred Jews occupied a disproportionately high percentage of the leading and most visible posts in the new governments.

The great exception to the pattern was Yugoslavia under the independent leadership of President Tito, a Croatian metal worker from Zagreb who became a Communist while a prisoner of war in Russia during the Bolshevik Revolution. Tito and his chief comrades—Edvard Kardelj, Milovan Djilas, Moshe Pijade—won Yugoslavia with little help from the Russians. The partisan forces they assembled and directed in the mountains during World War II were effective fighters against the Germans and Italians and also against the anti-Communist forces of the Chetnik leader, General Draja Mihailovich.

In building his guerrilla bands, Tito had cannily followed a united-front policy, welcoming all who would fight the enemy. He was also astute enough to win the reluctant support of the United States and Britain, which supplied him with large quantities of arms and other aid. In the last stages of the war the Red Army helped clear Yugoslavia of the Axis forces, but Tito could claim that his men had done most of the job. Unlike the Communist rulers elsewhere in Eastern Europe, Tito and his comrades had a self-confidence and independence born of the knowledge that they had won power themselves. Independent though they were, they were ardent supporters of Stalin, taking the lead in the region in setting up a state in which Communists alone held the reins of power.

As events proved, they had their illusions. Ardent Communists, they looked forward to doing their bit in communizing the world. They were also nationalists, eager to get as much territory out of the postwar settlement as possible. They had expected Moscow's support for their foreign-policy goals as well as its help in restoring the Yugoslav economy. On both scores they were mistaken, for they found that the Soviet Union was willing to compromise with the West on foreign-policy issues to serve its own ends and that it expected the Yugoslavs to put Soviet interests ahead of theirs when there was a conflict.

For three years after World War II Yugoslavia gave every sign of being one of the most loyal of Soviet satellites. Its propaganda dutifully echoed Soviet diatribes against the West. Hatred of the United States was inspired in 1946 with the downing of an American plane that strayed off course. But behind the scenes Soviet-Yugoslav tensions were developing.

In March 1948 all Soviet military and civilian advisers were ordered out of Yugoslavia. Three months later the quarrel exploded in public when the Communist Information Bureau—the "Cominform" set up late in 1947 to coordinate international Communist activities—announced the expulsion of Yugoslavia.

A resolution accused Tito and his comrades of being anti-Soviet, of using "brutal measures" against loyal, i.e., pro-Soviet, Communists in Yugoslavia and of creating "a disgraceful, purely Turkish terrorist regime." The resolution concluded with the demand that the Tito group rectify its mistakes and expressed confidence that if that did not happen, there were "healthy elements" in Yugoslavia that would replace Tito and his colleagues with "a new internationalist leadership of the party."

Stalin was confident that the Cominform action would do the job. As he said at the time: "I will shake my little finger —and there will be no more Tito." Stalin had made one of the greatest errors of his long career, for Tito did not fall. Instead, he used the Soviet-sponsored denunciation to bolster his support at home, appealing to the Yugoslavs' patriotism and appearing as the defender of national autonomy against Soviet imperialism. His real crime in Stalin's eyes, it appeared, was his independence and his nationalism.

The struggle during the next five years, until Stalin's death in 1953, was bitter, but Tito persisted. The Cominform excoriated him and his associates as imperialist agents who had betrayed Communism to the United States. Yugoslavia was branded as a capitalist state. The Communist countries on its borders became centers for political, economic, and propaganda warfare and the source of agents dispatched to try to overthrow the government. The Yugoslavs, heavily dependent on the other Communist countries for markets and supplies, were subjected to an economic blockade.

Out of Tito's defiance of Stalin grew the so-called National Communism and "revisionism" that have since plagued Moscow and the Communist world. Tito, insisting that he was still a Communist, maintained that the doctrine he stood for was a better and more faithful version of Marxism-Leninism than the tyrannies Stalin had imposed on the Soviet Union and the Eastern European countries under his control. The Yugoslav leader, freed of the compulsion to admire everything Russian and to imitate every Soviet institution, began to experiment, to introduce changes that might make his regime more popular and enable the society and the economy to function.

Not long after the break with Stalin he decided to end forced collectivization. The result was a mass exodus from the collective farms and the rebuilding of Yugoslav agriculture on the basis of small peasant holdings, assisted by cooperatives on the Scandinavian model that provided machinery and other necessities. Also abandoned was the Soviet planned economy which, in those days, attempted to direct all production from the center.

In its place Tito established what was called a socialist market economy, emphasizing the guidance of production by the forces of supply and demand in the market rather than by government planners. Yugoslav factories were directed to compete, to try to meet consumer needs and to make profits as a reward for satisfying their customers. Advertising was legalized and comic strips appeared in the newspapers. In the factories, power was theoretically given to democratically elected workers' councils, which were authorized to make key decisions and choose directors.

In those and other areas the Yugoslav leaders proclaimed their desire to create a democratic socialism far removed from the dictatorial Soviet model. True, the reforms were sometimes more evident in words than in deeds, and the Yugoslav Communists—joined in the renamed League of Yugoslav Communists—still retained final control. But the spirit of the changes was far different from the atmosphere of the Soviet Union.

Coming at the height of the Cold War hostility between the Soviet Union and the United States, Tito's revolt confused many in the West. Convinced that the central issue in the world was the struggle between Communism and capitalism, many Americans found it difficult to believe that a Communist leader could really break with Moscow. There was widespread suspicion that the whole affair was a ruse to victimize the West. Not until 1950 did the United States, Britain, and France decide that the revolt was genuine and that Tito should be helped. In the next few years, in a repetition of what had happened during the war, Yugoslavia received several billion dollars' worth of military and economic aid.

Tito's defection aroused Stalin's fear that there might be other potential Titos in Eastern Europe. The response was to purge the area's Communist parties in an effort to remove nationalistically minded leaders. In Bulgaria the chief victim was Traicho Kostov, a Deputy Premier, who was executed after a trial in which he was accused of defending Bulgarian economic interests too vigorously in trade negotiations with the Soviet Union. In Hungary the chief victim was a former Interior Minister, Laszlo Rajk, who "confessed" that he and his confederates had served as spies and saboteurs for Tito and the "American imperialists"; he was executed. In Czechoslovakia the former Communist party General Secretary, Rudolf Slansky, a Jew, and the former Minister of Foreign Affairs, Vlado Clementis, a Slovak, were the chief defendants in a major show trial. They "confessed" that they had spied for Tito and the United States Central Intelligence Agency as well as for Israel and "the world Zionist conspiracy"; they were executed.

Only in Poland was the life of the chief heretic spared. Wladyslaw Gomulka, who had earlier been Secretary General of the Communist party and is its head now, was given a long prison sentence for his nationalist views. Others who were imprisoned at the time but have emerged in pre-eminent political roles in recent years are Gustav Husak, a Slovak now head of the Czechoslovak Communist party, and Janos Kadar, now the Hungarian party leader.

Another aspect of the Tito-Stalin split is of consequence: its impact on Albania. From 1946 to 1948 Albania was essentially a satellite of the Yugoslavs, mainly dependent on them for technicians and for food and other essentials. There can be little doubt that Tito dreamed of annexing Albania; a start was made in November 1946, with an agreement providing for coordination of economic plans and currencies.

When the break between Yugoslavia and the Soviet Union came, the Albanian Communist leader, Enver Hoxha, decided to back Moscow. The chief Albanian scapegoat was the former Deputy Premier and Minister of the Interior, Koci Xoxe, who "confessed" at a trial that he was an agent for Tito who had tried to prepare the way for Albania's absorption into Yugoslavia; he was executed. The broader significance of the matter was Hoxha's demonstration that he regarded the preservation of Albania's independence as his prime objective.

Even among Communists there must be few who would deny that the early 1950's were a black time for the peoples of Soviet-dominated Eastern Europe. The death of Stalin provided an opportunity for them to vent their profound dissatisfaction with dictatorial governments and declining standards of living.

# 3

# The Explosions of 1953–1956

A SMALL-SCALE REVOLT broke out in the Czechoslovak city of Pilsen, home of the great Skoda Works, less than three months after Stalin's death in March 1953. According to the official radio, "rioters tore down pictures of Czech state leaders and hung up pictures of the imperialist agent Benes. The American gangsters [i.e., the rioters] stepped on pictures of Stalin and Gottwald and violated the Soviet flag. The archives in the town hall were burned." In some places the American flag was hoisted, and posters appeared with such legends as "Robbery Is the Russian Paradise."

The local police were able to end the disturbances without Soviet aid, but the restiveness pervading Eastern Europe had erupted. The immediate cause of the riots—a currency change that wiped out most savings—was peculiar to Czechoslovakia; the underlying mood was not.

Two weeks later on June 16 and 17, a much larger uprising broke out, this time in East Germany. The first spark was trivial, a strike by fewer than a hundred East Berlin building workers whose wages had been cut by a change in work rules.

Within hours the strike spread throughout East Germany. The next day tens of thousands of East Berliners went on a rampage, tearing down pictures of Stalin and Walter Ulbricht, the Communist leader, liberating prisoners, attacking secret policemen and Communist party officials, wrecking newspaper offices and even destroying the signs marking the border between East and West Berlin. By then the eruption, far beyond economic grievances, had become a political movement aimed at ending the Soviet occupation and at reunifying Germany. Moscow found this intolerable, of course, and Soviet tanks and troops were sent to put down the uprising. The revolt was soon crushed.

Something of a pattern had been set, and it was repeated in Hungary in 1956 and again in Czechoslovakia twelve years later. A vital element was United States inactivity. President Dwight D. Eisenhower and his Secretary of State, John Foster Dulles, had suggested they would "roll back" Soviet power in Eastern Europe, but when the test came they wanted no conflict with Moscow. Their inactivity erased any doubt that the United States implicitly recognized and accepted the Soviet sphere of influence in Eastern Europe, however much it might be denounced.

The available evidence suggests that the Kremlin leaders who succeeded Stalin were not surprised by the violence in Eastern Europe, for they knew they had inherited an unstable edifice of power. That knowledge inspired the policy of Stalin's first successor, Premier Georgi M. Malenkov, who promised rapid and substantial improvements in standards of living. Malenkov also understood that changes were essential in Eastern Europe if revolts were to be avoided.

Ironically, he had selected East Germany as the first nation in which to begin the retreat from Stalinist policies. Less than a week before the June uprising, in fact, major reforms directed by Moscow were announced by Ulbricht's regime. Thousands of political prisoners were ordered freed; the drive against the churches was halted; farmers were told they would not be forced into collectives, and there were concessions to more prosperous peasants.

In retrospect, it seems as if announcement of the reforms encouraged the revolt. Perhaps the unexpected retreat from Stalinism implied weakness, encouraging action by those East Germans who wanted to end Moscow's rule.

The Malenkov government was so intent on easing tensions that it did not let either the Czechoslovak incident or the East German explosion deter it from its course. It made major concessions to East Germany, canceling debts and promising new credits for the food and raw materials the East Germans needed.

A speech in Budapest in early July 1953 by the new Premier of Hungary demonstrated that the "new course" was not confined to East Germany and had not been halted by the uprising there. In the address, Imre Nagy, who emerged as the most powerful figure in Hungary after Stalin's death, sharply altered Hungarian economic policy. He declared that the economy was near collapse because the plan had set unrealistically difficult goals, taking no account of the lack of domestic raw materials. He called for a shift from emphasis on heavy industry to more rapid development of agriculture and of consumer goods production. Pressure on farmers to join collectives would end immediately, Nagy said, and farmers who had been forced to join would be allowed to leave. In the months that followed, the hold of the secret police on Hungary was lightened and many political prisoners were set free. The reversal of the policy Nagy's predecessor, Matyas Rakosi, had followed amounted to a peaceful revolution. Similar but much more limited retreats were subsequently announced in Rumania, Bulgaria, Czechoslovakia, and Poland.

The new course was not supported unanimously either in Moscow or in the Eastern European capitals. Behind the scenes forces in the Kremlin fought stubbornly to displace Malenkov and to reverse his policies. When he was ousted early in 1955, the move was widely regarded as a repudiation of the new course, and repercussions began to be felt in Eastern Europe. Shortly afterward, Nagy, whose version of the new course was the most extreme in Eastern Europe, was removed as Premier of Hungary; Rakosi, who had opposed the reforms, returned to power and began trying to put the clock back.

In Moscow and the other capitals, the battle between reformers and Stalinists continued, so that Eastern Europe presented an increasingly diverse picture of reform and retrogression. Perhaps the most important gain flowed from the decline of the secret police, a result of the Soviet purge of Lavrenti P. Beria, Stalin's security chief, whose execution had been announced late in 1953. But in the wake of Malenkov's ouster, some even feared that the old secret police repression would return.

The uncertainty about Moscow's post-Malenkov course did not last beyond the spring of 1955. It ended when Nikita S. Khrushchev, then First Secretary of the Soviet party and the man who had engineered Malenkov's downfall, turned out to be an anti-Stalinist, a leader who had united with the Stalinists in the Kremlin only temporarily to bring down Malenkov. By June 1955 Krushchev had made his own position sufficiently secure so as to begin to steal Malenkov's political clothes. He soon emerged as an advocate of the same reforms as the man he had deposed.

Khrushchev's policy became apparent when he moved to liquidate the quarrel with Tito in order to draw Yugoslavia back into line as an ally. Using his characteristically direct technique, he journeyed to Belgrade in mid-1955 and apologized to the Yugoslavs for the long campaign of psychological, political, and economic warfare against them. It was all Beria's fault, said Khrushchev, and since Beria was long since dead and disgraced, there was no obstacle to renewed friendship and ideological unity. Khrushchev underlined his belief that Yugoslavia was still a socialist state despite the many deviations from the Soviet model put into effect after 1948. Implied in all this was the acknowledgment that a true socialist society did not have to copy the Soviet Union slavishly but could adapt its institutions to local conditions and desires. In effect, he endorsed the idea that there were many roads to socialism.

The impact of Khrushchev's move on the rest of Eastern Europe was great and immediate. Millions interpreted the unprecedented apology as an admission that the Soviet Union had been politically defeated by Yugoslavia. Inevitably, throughout the region there was a tremendous upsurge in the prestige of Tito and his ideas as well as new respectability for the national Communists who had survived the ruthless Stalinist purges.

Pressure began building for emulation of the Yugoslavs and their independent foreign policy, their relatively great freedom of discussion and criticism, their workers' councils, their abolition of collective farms, and their reliance on market forces to guide much of the economy. In addition, ghosts of the past began to haunt the Eastern European governments. If Tito was not an American spy and agent, how then could Laszlo Rajk in Hungary or Rudolf Slansky in Czechoslovakia or other convicted "Titoist tools of American imperialism" have been guilty of the crimes for which they had been executed? The dead could not be brought to life again, protesters pointed out, but their reputations could be restored and their survivors could be compensated.

Moscow, aware that the cohesiveness of the Soviet bloc was loosening in this post-Stalin period, looked for means of improving the situation. The fear of a rearmed Germany, the Soviet leaders knew, was strong in Eastern Europe, and it was on this that they relied. Their opportunity was created by the decision of the Western Allies to permit West Germany to enter the North Atlantic Treaty Organization and to establish an army of limited size. To counter that, Moscow, in May 1955, called a Warsaw conference attended by all the Eastern European nations except Yugoslavia. From it emerged the Warsaw Pact—presented to the world as the Communist analogue of NATO—which formally united the armies of the Soviet Union and the Eastern European countries under a joint command. The armies were already under the Russians' control, of course; the Warsaw Pact gave them legal ground for keeping Soviet forces in Hungary and Rumania. It also enabled them to demand that Soviet troops be allowed to enter Warsaw Pact countries where they were not stationed, a demand justified by the pretext of conducting joint maneuvers.

One fruit of the post-Stalin liberalization was the lifting of some of the barriers that had hindered American journalists wishing to visit Eastern Europe. In September 1955, I was able to go to Warsaw and get a first-hand view of the new atmosphere.

On my first morning a leading Polish journalist took me on a guided tour of the capital. Then still in the throes of overcoming the enormous destruction of World War II, it offered vivid evidence of its inhabitants' past suffering and present hardships.

There were more positive aspects also. Every few minutes we passed another statue to another bygone hero, and my guide insisted upon stopping and telling me about many of them. One was a statue of a king who fought the Russians in the sixteenth century; another of a prince who directed a rebellion against the Russians in the nineteenth century; a third of a general who had defeated the Russian Army in some battle I had never heard of, and so on. I listened to the recital with growing amazement since I knew my companion was a trusted Communist. Finally I asked: "Are you trying to tell me that Warsaw's streets and squares are really a kind of permanent memorial to Poland's struggles against Russia?" He chuckled and replied: "Why do people in the West seem to forget that we who live in Poland today are just as much Poles as our ancestors were?"

Another Pole told me that a work called "A Poem for Adults," by Adam Wazyk, had caused a major sensation when it was published in a Warsaw newspaper. Here are some verses:

> . . . Unhuman Poland,
> howling with boredom on December nights . . .
> In garbage baskets and on hanging ropes,
> boys fly like cats on night walls,

burst with rutting—and then the "duchesses"
ditch the fetus—the Vistula flows here . . .
There are Polish apples unobtainable by Polish children,
there are children scorned by criminal doctors,
there are boys forced to lie,
there are girls forced to lie . . .
There are people waiting for justice,
there are people who have been waiting for a long time.

It was suggested that Wazyk had the Russians in mind
when he wrote:

. . . When the good people from the moon
refuse us the right to have taste,
it's true,
then we are in danger of becoming ignorant and dull.

That autumn in Eastern Europe there was a general revolt
of the intellectuals against Soviet domination and against the
humiliation and economic hardships which many Eastern
Europeans blamed on Moscow. Wazyk was not alone in
beginning to tell the truth about conditions a decade after the
Red Army had fastened Communist control on the region.
Here is how a young Hungarian poet, Karoly Jobbagy, described farm life in his country:

Don't talk to me about spaceships,
trips to the moon, Mars,
life in the atomic age . . .
The oxcarts sink in a shoreless sea of mud.
Our roads are mud, the farmyards, the pastures.
When winter comes, the rain beats like this,
And men, if they only could, would turn to beasts
and sleep, and see nothing.
Darkness comes early; there's no electricity here.
We sit beside a cold lamp; the mind sputters, vainly
sparking behind the skull.

A "poet's revolution" was taking place in Eastern Europe. It did not remain confined to poets, for they were articulating emotions and ideas burning in millions.

Much of the old fear of the Soviet Union had vanished and more people dared to voice, and even act on, their grievances. Objectively, conditions had improved appreciably—in terms of living standards and civil rights—since Stalin's death, but subjectively many people were even angrier than before since their aspirations went far beyond the degree of reform achieved. Indeed, they began to take for granted the changes that had seemed impossible while Stalin lived. Precisely because there had been such real and unexpected improvement, they began to demand more fundamental alterations in their situation. They began thinking of ending Soviet domination and creating representative governments.

Such was the psychological climate in Eastern Europe in February 1956, when Khrushchev delivered the most devastating blow to Stalin's reputation and, by implication, to the greater part of the Stalinist system that still remained unchanged or little changed. He portrayed the dictator as a paranoid psychopath who had murdered thousands of loyal Communists, brought the Soviet Union near the point of destruction and elevated himself to the status of a living god. Rather than being a god, Khrushchev made plain, Stalin was more like an insane devil.

The speech, originally made in secret to the Twentieth Congress of the Soviet Communist party, did not remain secret for long. The Central Intelligence Agency obtained a copy and the State Department made it public. The effect in Eastern Europe was powerful. Millions learned that they had been systematically and cynically lied to for a decade; those who had believed most ardently in Communism and, therefore, in Stalin were the most disillusioned. Throughout Eastern Europe the speech stirred contempt for a system that had permitted itself to be run for so long by a monster.

With the new attitude toward the Soviet system came revulsion against the Eastern European leaders who had been Stalin's puppets. More and more people at every level decided that Tito was the model that should be followed—a model based on defiance of the Soviet Union and defense of national interests.

It was no great surprise, then, when a political tornado struck Eastern Europe between June and November of 1956. The first explosion, in Poznan, Poland, represented a small-scale, spontaneous revolt; beginning with demands for better wages and living conditions, it soon expanded to calls for restoration of freedom and genuine independence. The revolt was quickly suppressed by armed force, but within a few weeks it became increasingly evident that the "rioters" had won a moral victory. Their demands were publicized and discussed approvingly in the Polish press and other media. By midsummer dangerous and open tension flared between Poland and the Soviet Union as Moscow protested in vain against the subversive ideas being expressed. The Communist rulers of Poland found themselves endangered on two fronts—on one side the rising nationalistic anger of the people, who scented an opportunity to win genuine independence; on the other the Kremlin's fear that the situation might be getting out of control. The mood of the people indicated revolution on a scale dwarfing what had happened in Poznan; the Kremlin threatened military action by the thousands of Soviet troops in Poland.

In the search for a way out, Poland's leaders turned to

Wladyslaw Gomulka, who had been secretly released from prison in 1955. The fact that he had been imprisoned for his nationalist views gave him incomparable prestige; the fact that he was a Communist held hope that he might be able to reach a compromise with Moscow. The Kremlin would not be pleased by Gomulka's elevation, the Poles knew, but Mao Tse-tung encouraged them to be bold, giving them secret assurances that China would support greater national self-assertion in Poland.

Gomulka was elected head of the Polish Socialist Workers (Communist) party in October. Just before Gomulka's election, Khrushchev and other Soviet leaders flew to Warsaw to protest. In a dramatic confrontation with the Polish leaders, the visitors threatened armed action to prevent what they regarded as a betrayal. But the Poles stood their ground, warning that Soviet military action would mean war. Khrushchev retreated and accepted Gomulka's elevation as part of a compromise Soviet-Polish agreement.

These events were greeted by the Poles with delirious joy. The "Polish October" was viewed as a new spring, the equivalent of a successful revolution that had ended Soviet rule and opened the way for meeting the people's demands for a better and freer life.

Initially Gomulka encouraged such hopes, denouncing the repression and economic hardships of the past, revealing that the country was virtually insolvent and promulgating major reforms. The most important reforms were new freedom for the Roman Catholic Church and the end of enforced collectivization. Soviet citizens who held major posts in the government, notably the Defense Minister, Marshal Konstantin K. Rokossovsky, a Pole by birth, resigned their positions and went back to Moscow. Not since Tito broke with Stalin had Eastern Europe seen such dramatic and radical change.

The Polish developments were soon overshadowed by even more dramatic events in Hungary. Four days after Khrushchev backed down in his confrontation with Gomulka, the Hungarians revolted. The uprising briefly ended the Communist monopoly of power and sought to prepare the way for the conversion of Hungary into a neutral, democratic state on the model of Austria. But the Red Army invaded Hungary and after a series of bloody clashes in Budapest and elsewhere, reimposed Moscow's dominance.

The uprising was the culmination of Hungarian dissidence that had been manifesting itself since 1953. That dissidence had received new impetus from Khrushchev's denunciation of Stalin and from the news that the Twentieth Party Congress had rehabilitated Bela Kun, leader of the short-lived first Hungarian Communist regime just after World War I, whom Stalin had executed as a spy in 1937. Then the Petofi Circle, a discussion group of intellectuals, began meeting in Budapest, attracting thousands to hear denunciations of Communist misrule. A typical speech was made by the widow of Laszlo Rajk, who said after her husband's "rehabilitation":

"Comrades, I stand before you deeply moved after five years of prison and humiliation. Let me tell you this: So far as prisons are concerned, in Horthy's prisons conditions were far better even for Communists than in Rakosi's prisons. Not only was my husband killed, but my little baby was torn from me; for years, I received no letters and no information about the fate of my little son.

"These criminals have not only murdered Laszlo Rajk. They have trampled underfoot all sentiment and honesty in this country. Murderers should not be criticized—they should be punished. I shall never rest until those who have ruined the country, corrupted the party, destroyed thousands and driven millions into despair receive their just punishments! Comrades, help me in this struggle!"

The Soviet leaders tried to ease the tension by ousting Rakosi. Soviet Politburo member Anastas I. Mikoyan, the shrewd Armenian politician, flew to Budapest to order the elevation of Erno Gero, an old Rakosi associate who, Moscow hoped, might turn the tide of dissatisfaction. Gero also proved helpless because Rakosi's downfall merely encouraged the dissenters. Visitors to Hungary could see the old pattern of Communist rule melting away before their eyes.

It was characteristic of the period that when a delegation of Hungarian writers went to Yugoslavia, they were not impressed. At that moment in history, they reported, there was more freedom in Hungary than in Yugoslavia. At home, they added, there was no longer a "cult of personality" such as that surrounding Tito, whose picture was visible everywhere. (A year earlier, it should be added, it would have seemed fantastic to Hungarians that they should enjoy even half the freedom of the Yugoslavs.)

The upsurge of anger and hope found dramatic expression on October 6, 1956, when hundreds of thousands of Hungarians participated in an enormously impressive and moving memorial to Rajk, in which his remains were removed from a traitor's grave and placed beside the heroes of their history. Even so, no fundamental changes were made by Gero or his masters in Moscow.

The revolution began on October 23, as a series of demonstrations expressing solidarity with Poland. The demonstrators went on to demand that Nagy be returned to power, that Rakosi and his supporters be put on trial and that the Soviet Army leave. Demonstrations turned into revolution when the secret police, defending the Gero government, killed several demonstrators. The result was an orgy of violence directed first and foremost against the Communist party, the secret police, and all those held responsible for the nation's sufferings. The huge statue of Stalin in Budapest was pulled down; party headquarters and bookstores were burned to the ground; secret police officials were lynched. When Soviet units joined in shooting at the demonstrators, further violence resulted.

Desperate to damp down an explosive situation, the Russians turned to Nagy, had him named Premier and tried to use him to calm a people venting long-repressed grievances. The Soviet Army was withdrawn from the capital. But no mere change of personalities and conciliation could save the situation; nor could the people forget that Russians had shot Hungarians. Nagy, under strong pressure from the public, was compelled to make far more drastic changes than he had first contemplated.

A multiparty coalition government was formed in which officials in the long-banned Smallholders, Peasant, and Social Democratic parties were given ministerial posts.

Political prisoners were set free, among them Joszef Cardinal Mindszenty, long-imprisoned head of the Roman Catholic Church in Hungary, to whom all civil and ecclesiastical rights were restored. Throughout the country the remaining collective farms dissolved almost overnight and workers' councils were set up in the factories. Within two weeks the new government was demanding that Hungary be allowed to withdraw from the Warsaw Pact, that it be recognized as a neutral state on a par with Austria and that Soviet troops leave permanently. Hungary's borders to the West, long closed and tightly guarded, were opened.

It was all too good to last, of course. The Soviet leaders had no intention of letting Hungary regain sovereignty and freedom. They recognized that just as the Hungarian revolution had gained strength from the Soviet retreat in Poland, so a capitulation in Hungary would prepare the way for the loss of the rest of Eastern Europe.

It was also evident in those tense days that initially the Kremlin sought to avoid using the crudest instruments of power. *Pravda* published a government declaration acknowledging that there had been "downright mistakes" in relations among Communist countries and promising reforms. But it was too late for words to save the situation. On November 4 the Soviet Army attacked in Budapest and other Hungarian cities. There was no advance warning and the odds were unequal. Nevertheless, the Hungarians fought as best they could against the tanks, the machine guns, the artillery, and the planes. Thousands were killed or wounded but the end was inevitable: the Soviet Army became the master of Hungary once again.

Nagy and his closest collaborators were arrested after being tricked by the promise of safe conduct into leaving the Yugoslav Embassy, where they had taken refuge. Nagy was later executed. Tens of thousands of Hungarians fled abroad in despair.

There were angry editorials in the Western press and the Soviet Union was denounced bitterly in speeches at the United Nations—but at the crucial time no nation had come forward to help the Hungarians.

Moscow, never acknowledging that it had simply invaded, took care to provide a political cover for its actions. It gathered a group of Hungarian Communists under the leadership of Janos Kadar and had them proclaim a Hungarian Revolutionary Worker-Peasant government. No one had authorized them to do so nor could they point to a single large group of their countrymen who supported them or even knew in advance of their action. But it was in the name of this "government" that the Russians attacked. When the battle was over Kadar was installed as the successor to Rakosi, Gero, and Nagy.

Ironically, Kadar had suffered under Rakosi, having been sent to prison and, it is said, tortured. His background, Moscow hoped, would eventually make him acceptable. Moreover, the Kadar group took care to announce a program that would appeal to Hungarians, promising to raise the standard of living quickly and substantially, to guarantee democratic elections and, after the restoration of peace and order, to negotiate on the withdrawal of Soviet troops.

Soviet forces are still in Hungary.

From Moscow's point of view the compromise in Poland and the crushing of the Hungarian revolution saved Eastern Europe. But the Kremlin, recognizing the rebellious mood in its colonies, decided to make still more concessions. Old debts were canceled, substantial economic aid was poured into the area to permit improvement of the standard of living, and the governments were informed that they could have more independence in domestic policy. As long as the Communist parties remained in control and as long as they fully supported Soviet foreign policy, they could adapt the

Soviet model to meet local needs with a relatively wide degree of freedom.

Implicit in all this was the warning that the Eastern Europeans should not go too far in copying the Yugoslav system. Moreover, Yugoslav-Soviet relations became embittered again after the suppression of the Hungarians. Soon Soviet spokesmen were once more attacking the Yugoslav system as a deviation from Marxism-Leninism.

With the wisdom of hindsight and the knowledge of what happened in Prague in 1968, the question arises: Why did Czechoslovakia remain so passive in 1956, when its participation would have linked Poland and Hungary, making Moscow's intervention that much more difficult? When I asked Czechs and Slovaks why they had stayed aloof, they replied somewhat shamefacedly more or less as follows: The country was still too prosperous then—still enjoying the dividends from its superior industrialization—to be seriously concerned with revolt. The anger manifested in Pilsen in 1953 was not widespread. Furthermore, there were historic reasons for many Czechs and Slovaks to harbor anti-Polish and anti-Hungarian feelings.

Bitter voices in Eastern Europe declared that in 1956 the Hungarians had acted like Poles, daring to fight for freedom against impossible odds; the Poles had acted like Czechs, calculating their actions carefully and trying to avoid undue risks, while the Czechs had acted like dogs. Memories of Czechoslovakia's passivity in 1956 may have played a role in shaping the 1968 policies of Hungary and Poland, which participated in the suppression of the Prague uprising then.

In any case, Czechoslovakia's pro-Soviet conduct in 1956

53

must be traced to Antonin Novotny, then dictator in Prague. A former locksmith, a man of colorless personality with no oratorical talent and an absence of intellectual interests, he was above all an expert *apparatchik,* a consummate master of the in-fighting in the Communist bureaucracy.

He became boss of Czechoslovakia in 1953 after Klement Gottwald's death. There is reason to suppose that his elevation was in part a reward for his role in arranging the frame-up of Rudolf Slansky, Vladimir Clementis, and the other defendants in the 1952 purge trial. Novotny blocked excessive repercussions from Khrushchev's unsettling moves by keeping the lid of secret-police control on as tightly as possible. True, he allowed a little public ventilation of intellectuals' discontent in 1956 and he purged Gottwald's son-in-law, Alexei Cepicka, as a symbol of his anti-Stalinism. Nevertheless tight Stalinist repression continued. Stalin's statue may have been pulled down in Budapest, but in Prague it still stood high on a hilltop overlooking the city.

Rumania also remained quiet in 1956 under the dictatorial control of Gheorghe Gheorghiu-Dej. Judged by the limitations on free speech and other civil rights, it was one of the most Stalinist countries in Eastern Europe and remained so well into the 1960's. Gheorghiu-Dej apparently argued behind the scenes in 1956, as he did later in public, that he had dealt with the Stalinism issue in 1952 when he removed Ana Pauker and her key associates from political power. His basic rule, which worked, was that incipient discontent was best checked by never allowing it to be expressed.

In Bulgaria the problems posed by Khrushchev's war on Stalinism were met by the controlled release of some tension. The "Stalin of Bulgaria," Premier Vulko Chervenkov, was demoted, though he remained a man of considerable power.

Steps were taken to relax the old atmosphere of terror, to strengthen "socialist legality" and to improve living standards. But the reforms were small and owed little or nothing to widespread discontent or to pressure from intellectuals like that in Poland and Hungary.

The Soviet Union could congratulate itself that it had preserved its Eastern European empire—that a combination of compromise and harsh military action had warded off the worst threats. The cost had been high, since far more autonomy had had to be granted to the Eastern Europeans, along with substantial if temporary subsidies.

Khrushchev may have consoled himself that the worst was over. If so he missed the significance of a most important new feature on the Eastern European landscape: Premier Chou En-lai traveling in late 1956 and early 1957 from one Eastern European country to another to throw China's weight on the side of conciliation between Moscow and its satellites. For the first time since the Mongol invasion in the thirteenth century an Asian power had begun to play a substantial role in European politics.

# 4

# Eastern Europe
# Under Khrushchev

IN A FACTORY dining room in Bucharest on a June morning in 1962, I watched with astonishment as Premier Khrushchev humiliated and scolded the Rumanian Communist chief, Gheorghe Gheorghiu-Dej. Khrushchev was on an official visit, and a large group of newspapermen was following the Soviet and Rumanian leaders as they inspected the factory. The dining room appeared beautiful, especially the tables with bright blue cloths and vases of spring flowers.

Khrushchev stopped and said, "I wonder what's underneath these tablecloths." With his hamlike hand he swept off flowers and cloth, exposing an old, rickety table discolored by years of use and abuse. Furious, Khrushchev turned on his host and exclaimed: "For me there are all these pretty things"—he gestured at the decoration—"but for the workers there is only this trash!" He pointed contemptuously at the table.

The Soviet leaders were usually meticulous in the courtesy and respect they extended to Eastern European leaders in public, yet Khrushchev had treated Gheorghiu-Dej like an incompetent office boy. During the week that followed Khrushchev, normally an ebullient man full of jokes and earthy sayings, became surly and tight-lipped, going through the unavoidable formalities as quickly as possible and then hiding from public view.

Not for many months did Western reporters understand that they had witnessed the first signs of the bitter behind-the-scenes conflict between the Soviet and Rumanian leaders. Khrushchev was furious not only because the Rumanians were defying his wishes but also because he felt they had tricked him. In 1958, confident of their loyalty and subservience, he had withdrawn all Soviet troops; from that time on they became increasingly recalcitrant and independent-minded.

When Khrushchev rebuked Gheorghiu-Dej their disputes centered on economic issues. The Rumanians wanted to build a comprehensive industrial complex, including steel plants and an auto factory. The Russians opposed those ambitions, arguing that Rumania did not need large-scale heavy industry and should concentrate on agriculture and oil production.

There was a bitter dispute, too, on the future of the Council for Mutual Economic Assistance, to which all the Soviet-dominated countries in Eastern Europe still belonged. Khrushchev, who wanted to use Comecon to unify the Soviet Bloc economically, proposed that one comprehensive plan govern the Soviet Union and the Eastern European satellites —a plan that would control development and resources without regard for national boundaries.

The Rumanians, objecting bitterly, insisted that only their government could control Rumanian resources. They threatened to veto the proposal, a course open to them because

Stalin had framed Comecon's rules to require that decisions be unanimous (presumably he wanted to give the appearance of equality between the Soviet Union and its satellites, on the assumption that no Eastern European country would dare act against Soviet wishes). Eventually the Rumanians vetoed the comprehensive economic plan.

Subsequently Rumania went even further in asserting its independence. It abolished the compulsory teaching of Russian in the schools, ended the pre-eminence of Soviet books, movies, and plays, and gave Rumanian names to streets that had been named for Soviet heroes. Nevertheless, it remained in the Soviet bloc's military alliance, the Warsaw Pact, and in Comecon.

The Rumanians, extremely methodical in their revolt against Soviet domination, usually took only one cautious step at a time, always striving to avoid sensational actions that would catch the attention of the foreign press. Publicly, the government did not differ with the Soviet Union; Rumanian foreign-policy statements at the United Nations dutifully echoed the Moscow line. The dominant position of the Communist party was carefully preserved and there were far fewer domestic concessions to liberal trends than Khrushchev had granted in the Soviet Union. But on one point there was no yielding: the leaders in Bucharest would decide their policy and would not sacrifice Rumanian interests to those of the Soviet Union.

Rumania's emergence as an increasingly independent fortress of national Communism signified the failure of Khrushchev's post-1956 policy. The Soviet leader, having crushed the Hungarian revolt and compromised with the Polish dissidents under Gomulka, sought to knit the Eastern European countries closer to Moscow by treating them more liberally than Stalin had. Moreover, he began to confer with the Eastern European leaders to hammer out common positions, seeking to give the impression that their interests and preferences were being considered along with those of the Soviet Union.

In the initial stages the Rumanian drive for increased independence must have seemed no more threatening to Moscow than the growing diversity exhibited by more loyal Eastern European countries. The question then arises: Why did Khrushchev allow the Rumanians to defy him in the early 1960's since he had adequate precedent, if he needed any, for energetic action against heretics? The reason for his restraint, it is clear, was the new factor—Communist China —in the situation in Eastern Europe.

The Chinese, as we have noted, encouraged the Poles to defy Moscow in 1956. Then Premier Chou toured the region in an apparent effort to help reduce the tensions between the Eastern Europeans and Moscow. The very fact of his intervention implied a claim to influence in Eastern Europe, and a challenge to the Soviet monopoly of power.

Whatever Chou's purpose, discord persisted between the Soviet and Chinese leaders, for the Chinese saw Khrushchev's attack on Stalin as a covert attack on Mao Tse-tung and *his* cult of personality. The Chinese were also angered by Khrushchev's emphasis on peaceful coexistence and they resented the fact that he gave priority to improvements in the Soviet standard of living and to increases in Soviet economic strength rather than to the cause of world revolution.

Furthermore, the Chinese were annoyed because Khrushchev had refused to give them more economic aid and to acknowledge that much of Russia's territory in Asia was stolen from the Chinese Empire by the czars. Not least, Mao was embittered by Khrushchev's effort to succeed Stalin as the chief lawgiver of world Communism even though the Soviet leader had accomplished nothing comparable to Mao's historic feat of leading the party to victory in China.

Recurrent efforts to patch up the differences failed, and by 1960, though the world knew little about the growing breach, the two countries had become bitter rivals. Both sought allies among other countries and parties, with the Chinese scoring a major coup by winning over the Albanians in 1960.

Albania's decision to side with Mao against Khrushchev was based on self-interest. Hoxha and his comrades had watched with growing uneasiness as relations between the Soviet Union and Yugoslavia improved after Stalin's death despite the temporary discord after the Hungarian revolt. From the Albanian point of view China seemed an ideal protector. Large enough so that it could supply the economic and technical assistance that Albania needed, it was also powerful enough so that the Russians would be reluctant to mount any military move against the Albanians. In addition, the Chinese had a major ideological quarrel with the Yugoslavs because Mao saw Tito's economic innovations as a return to capitalism.

As a result of the new alignment, Soviet relations with Albania became strained and they were finally broken in December 1961. Earlier that year Soviet submarines were forced to vacate a naval base on Albanian territory and Khrushchev withdrew all his technical specialists and canceled economic aid.

At the Twenty-second Congress of the Soviet Communist party in October 1961, Khrushchev made the dispute public. He astonished the world by denouncing the Albanian Communist leaders as a band of murderers and cutthroats who had established a reign of terror. In what seemed like a repetition of Stalin's vain efforts to overthrow Tito, Khrushchev called on the Albanian Communist rank and file to displace the Hoxha group.

The Chinese made it plain that they would support Hoxha. Chou En-lai, who headed the Chinese delegation at the Moscow meeting, devoted much of his address to the party congress to criticism of the Soviet leadership on the ground that the airing of the quarrel violated the principles of Marxism-Leninism and the code of behavior among Communist parties. He then left before the session was over. And Chinese ships carrying supplies and specialists began to arrive in Albania.

The Albanian situation helped the Rumanians to win increasing latitude. Locked in the struggle with China, Khrushchev wanted as much support as possible and feared that if he put too much pressure on the Rumanians, they might support the Chinese. For their part, the Rumanians maintained a neutral stance, insisting that they favored maximum unity among Communists and wanted to remain friendly with all. By implication, they were warning Moscow that any dramatic move or pressure would damage Communist unity and give the Chinese ammunition for anti-Soviet propaganda.


Khrushchev's policies were more successful elsewhere in Eastern Europe. In return for the increased freedom he was willing to allow, he received more voluntary cooperation. Poland, Hungary, Czechoslovakia, and Bulgaria welcomed his moves to ease international tension, to encourage contacts with the West and to permit greater diversity in intellectual and artistic life.

The most complex pattern of change during the Khrushchev era can be traced in Poland. Gomulka, it will be recalled, came to power on a wave of bitter anti-Soviet feeling. His chief credentials were that he opposed slavish subservience to Moscow in the late 1940's and had been imprisoned for his nationalism. Once in power, moreover, he made changes that responded to popular aspirations. Peasants were freed from the collective farms and allowed to cultivate their smallholdings. The Roman Catholic Church was permitted to function on a scale and with a freedom matched by no other formal religious body in the Communist world. Gomulka was also able to avail himself of American economic aid and of special privileges denied most other Communist countries, for exports to the United States.

On balance, nonetheless, Gomulka disappointed many who had supported him in 1956; liberals felt betrayed and spoke of "the retreat from October." Aiming to assure Moscow of Poland's loyalty, the party leader devoted much energy to suppressing the most liberal and anti-Soviet forces. He also made sure that the press, the radio, and television toed the party line. However, he did not restore the police repression of the Stalin era, and people conceded that they could say anything they liked among themselves. But periodically conflict flared as Gomulka sought to curb the Roman Catholic Church and to limit its activity.

Gomulka maintained that his policy of cooperation with the Soviet Union was indispensable to the welfare of the country, caught as it was between the Soviet Union and Germany. He pointed out that much of Poland's post-World War II territory had been taken from Germany and that many German nationalists had not reconciled themselves to the loss, so that Poland had to rely on Soviet support. What Gomulka did not discuss was the nightmare that terrified many Polish nationalists: the possibility that a Soviet-German deal at Poland's expense might force the Poles to return the former German territories without being compensated.

Janos Kadar pursued a tough pro-Soviet policy after he was installed in Hungary by the Russians, purging those who had participated in the revolt. Symbolic of his harsh policy was the execution of Imre Nagy, who had been Premier at the height of the movement for freedom and who had tried to withdraw Hungary from the Warsaw Pact. But for the long run, Kadar recognized that his control had to rest on more solid foundations than Soviet bayonets: he had to win the support of the people and overcome their bitterness against the brutal Soviet repression.

In the first stages he emphasized improvements in living standards. Budapest in the early 1960's, I found, boasted an amazing number of beauty parlors and pastry shops. The American ambassador's wife said that she could always find good American cosmetics; one could never be sure which brands would be available but some were always on sale. A Communist regime that spent precious foreign exchange on American beauty aids was plainly quite different from the austere Stalinist model.

Kadar, going even further, in the early 1960's announced a policy summarized in the slogan: "He who is not against us is with us." This was an expression of confidence that he had won the support of most Hungarians and could trust ordinary citizens who had no record of active political opposition. It was also an effort to give more people a chance to

63

win responsible and desirable jobs based on ability, rather than only on party membership.

When I visited Budapest there were many tales of incompetent party members being ousted from key jobs and replaced by trained nonmembers. Kadar seemed to be winning popular support and overcoming the impression that he was merely Moscow's puppet.

A visitor to Prague in the late 1950's and early 1960's encountered an atmosphere of fear far more intense than anywhere else in Eastern Europe. Antonin Novotny, both President and head of the party, maintained perhaps the most Stalinist regime in the region. Even cabdrivers were unwilling to talk politics, sweeping a finger across the throat to signify what could happen to anyone caught deviating from the party line. The rigid censorship of the press was reflected in the boring "news"; as a result, most people seemed interested only in sports. There were even reports that Novotny had rebuffed suggestions from Khrushchev that he permit some liberalization. Almost the only visible sign of greater freedom was the increasing number of foreign tourists in Prague, and they could be explained primarily by a critical need for Western currencies with which to buy machinery and other essentials the Soviet Union could not supply.

The frozen situation reflected the fact that in 1956, when so many liberalizing changes took place elsewhere in Eastern Europe as well as in the Soviet Union, Novotny was able to contain and then destroy what little dissidence there was. But by the early 1960's pressure for change was beginning to develop, particularly over shortages of meat and other essentials. Walking the streets of Prague, one could tell where the butcher shops were by the long lines of impatient people, worried whether the supply would last.

Another center of dissatisfaction thrived among the bitter and restive Slovak intellectuals, who believed that the Prague leaders had repudiated promises of Slovak autonomy in a unified Czechoslovakia. Most Slovak intellectuals saw Novotny as a ruthless Czech dictator crushing a helpless Slovakia. In response they began demanding that the purge trials be re-examined and that martyred Slovak leaders, notably Vladimir Clementis, be cleared of charges of treason. By 1964 the Slovaks had gained much ground; Clementis was quietly rehabilitated and Slovak prisoners were freed.

Then, slowly but surely, the Stalinist style began to dissipate and censorship was eased. On the other hand, the secret police remained vigilant and Novotny's dictatorship changed little although it became somewhat less brutal in its techniques. Dissatisfaction continued to grow because the economy operated poorly—in one year the government had to admit that industrial production had declined, an almost-unheard-of event in the Soviet bloc—and the small increase of freedom whetted appetites for more. Greater contact with the West through tourism showed many Czechoslovaks how badly their country was doing economically. A man in Prague told me angrily that he had been shocked to discover that the standard of living in Vienna was much higher than in Prague although the two cities had been on a par before World War II.

Except for Albania, Bulgaria was the most backward, least industrialized Eastern European country during the Khrushchev era. Because it had a more genuine pro-Russian tradition than its neighbors, Moscow had little difficulty ensuring

65

its loyalty. Almost the only major sign of divergence appeared in 1960 when the leadership tried briefly to sponsor "a great leap forward" similar to that of the Chinese. Their effort to work miracles of economic growth overnight proved as unsuccessful as China's. Bulgaria had to content itself with its assigned role as the winter garden of the Soviet bloc —the source of early fruits and vegetables—while accepting industrialization that focused increasingly on supplying parts for Soviet-made machinery. The "specialization" was the essence of the "colonial economy" against which the Rumanians had successfully rebelled.

Bulgarian politics was dominated by the struggle between Vulko Chervenkov, the local Stalin in the early 1950's, Anton Yugov, who was Premier in the late 1950's and early 1960's, and Todor Zhivkov, the Communist party chief and eventual victor. Chervenkov's demotion in April 1956, a first effort at de-Stalinization, accomplished little and he remained among the powerful. Zhivkov was finally able to oust Chervenkov and Yugov in a second de-Stalinization wave in 1961–1962, but that testified more to Zhivkov's vigorous support by Moscow than to any basic difference between him and his foes.

During the Khrushchev era Yugoslavia continued to forge ahead on its independent path. It sought to strengthen its "self-management system" in the economy, to build up voluntary cooperatives—quite different from collective farms—among small peasants, to increase freedom of speech and press, and to improve relations between the nationalities that make up its uneasily diverse population. There was relatively rapid economic growth and living standards improved significantly.

Problems existed along with progress. The secret police continued to play an active role, making a mockery of the more exaggerated claims of Yugoslav democracy. The arrest and imprisonment of Milovan Djilas, the fiery Macedonian who was once Tito's close associate and possible successor, demonstrated the limits on freedom. Djilas's crime was the publication abroad of his book *The New Class,* a scorching portrayal of the new Communist elite, in which he argued that the old Yugoslav ruling class, drawn from royalty, the urban capitalists, and large landowners, had simply been replaced by a group that was exploiting the Communist victory for self-enrichment and self-advancement.

There was enough freedom of expression to permit the revelation that relations among the Yugoslav nationalities were still prickly and difficult. In particular, people in the poorest areas in the south believed that they were not getting enough help to industrialize rapidly and to raise their living standards to the levels prevailing among the more prosperous Croats and Slovenes in the north. The northerners, in turn, resented being heavily taxed for capital investment in the underdeveloped areas of Serbia, Macedonia and Bosnia and Herzegovina. That investment, the northerners felt, was often wasted because the southerners were inexperienced and ignorant about the construction and operation of new industrial plants.

In foreign policy Tito steered a complex course. He sought to maintain good relations with the United States, Britain, and France, which had helped him against Stalin and whose help he might need again, but he regarded himself as a faithful Communist and did not hesitate to denounce American foreign policy.

Yugoslav relations with Moscow, greatly improved after

Khrushchev's visit and apology, deteriorated sharply in the late 1950's, partly because of Yugoslav criticism of the invasion of Hungary in 1956. For a time Moscow denounced Yugoslavia's efforts to combine socialist ownership with market direction of the economy. But as the Soviet-Chinese dispute got worse, Khrushchev and Tito mended relations, trade increased, and some Soviet economic aid began moving to Yugoslavia again.

Tito's main interest was his dream of winning world stature through the organization and leadership of a bloc of nonaligned nations, a new third force standing between Moscow and Washington and pursuing an independent policy. It has not become the force he hoped it would be but he has continued to pursue his goal.

After the June 1953 revolt, Walter Ulbricht successfully maintained peace in East Germany. Backed fully by Moscow, which did not like the possibilities revealed by the uprising, he also warded off the challenges to his authority from ambitious younger associates. The greatly reduced rate of Soviet exactions from the East German economy permitted a steady if slow rise in living standards. Yet during the late 1950's and the early 1960's this progress was overshadowed by the phenomenally rapid economic growth of West Germany. Moreover, to maintain authority, Ulbricht retained more of the repressive Stalinist apparatus and practices than did most of the rulers of other Communist nations.

In short, East Germany was a less attractive place in which to live and work than West Germany, and year after year hundreds of thousands fled to West Germany through West Berlin. Since many were skilled workers, engineers, doctors, and other trained personnel, the steady loss was a serious drain on the East German economy.

To end the mass exodus there would have to be a fundamental change in Berlin. Khrushchev's first thought was to exert pressure on the Western Allies to withdraw their troops from West Berlin and convert it into a "free city." His demand, first voiced in November 1958, precipitated a major world crisis that for a time threatened to set off World War III. But the Western Allies stood firm and Khrushchev never dared carry out his implied threats.

In the summer of 1961 a simpler solution for the problem was found: The East Germans erected the Berlin Wall, which cut off East Berlin—and therefore East Germany—from West Berlin. Overnight the ready exit to freedom was gone for all except the handful who risked death by trying to scale the wall. Although the Western Allies protested they took no significant retaliatory action. Those who remained in East Germany faced the fact that if they wanted a better future they had to create it at home. The result was an intensification of economic development, a rapid rise in production, and a slow but notable improvement in living standards. It was the wall and its political and economic consequences that assured the survival of East Germany and finally forced West Germany to acknowledge in 1970 that it must recognize the German Democratic Republic politically.

# 5

# "Socialism with a Human Face"

SOMETHING CLOSE to panic struck the rulers of Eastern Europe in October 1964, when Nikita S. Khrushchev was unexpectedly replaced by the Brezhnev-Kosygin team. For a few days there was token moral resistance from Antonin Novotny and Wladyslaw Gomulka, who expressed astonishment and demanded explanations. Their reaction was understandable. The pro-Soviet Eastern European leaders had reached or retained power because of accommodations with Khrushchev; inevitably they wondered whether his fate presaged their own fall. The new Communist party chief, Leonid I. Brezhnev, and Premier Aleksei N. Kosygin, gave them immediate reassurance. At the same time Brezhnev and Kosygin, hoping to improve Moscow's position in Eastern Europe, sought to end Albania's links with China, to restrict Rumania's assertive independence, and to draw Yugoslavia closer to the Soviet Union. Their aim was to maintain Soviet dominance while encouraging economic development. In the period that followed, however, they encountered new disruptions, requiring difficult and even dangerous decisions.

"Socialism with a Human Face"

The new leaders in the Kremlin contributed to their own troubles when they undertook in 1965 to reform the Soviet economy. Their changes were comparatively modest, emphasizing increased incentives through profits and greater opportunities for plant managers to exercise initiative. The primacy of central planning was left unchanged, nor did the reformers envision anything as radical as the Yugoslav system of market socialism.

Limited as the Soviet changes were, they encouraged would-be reformers in Eastern Europe, many of whom advocated even more radical departures from the system of detailed central economic planning. In Czechoslovakia and Hungary, the Soviet reforms strengthened the position of liberal elements seeking political as well as economic change. Ota Sik, a Czechoslovak, and others argued that economic liberalization would not work unless accompanied by political liberalization that would encourage greater initiative.

The interest in reform had practical origins. Not only had the area's economic growth slowed, but increased contact with the West had shown the Eastern European leaders that the Soviet bloc was seriously behind in technology as well as in living standards. The need to improve performance and become more competitive with the West led to willingness to take the risks connected with the economic reforms. But the reforms automatically introduced strife because many veteran Communists felt that they smacked of "capitalism"; indeed, Chinese Communist propaganda asserted that the reforms *were* capitalism. Moreover, many bureaucrats in Eastern Europe saw their positions threatened since the changes put a premium on ability and ingenuity rather than on following orders and on party loyalty.

Another important source of friction was the six-day Middle East war in 1967. When the Israelis easily defeated their Arab neighbors despite the vast military assistance Moscow had given to the United Arab Republic and Syria, Soviet prestige in Eastern Europe suffered a serious decline. Those Eastern European governments that had followed Moscow's lead in breaking diplomatic relations with Israel and supporting the Arabs were similarly affected; they also encountered great dissatisfaction at home. (Rumania, alone in the region in adopting a neutral position and maintaining relations with Israel, gained in stature.)

To many Eastern Europeans the rapid and automatic manner in which their governments followed the Soviet lead was a humiliating reminder that their countries did not dare make independent foreign-policy decisions, as Rumania did. That reaction, widespread throughout the region, was strongest in Poland, where the government purged key military and political officials for their pro-Israel views, and in Czechoslovakia, where leading intellectuals turned a mid-1967 congress of the Czechoslovak Writers Union into what almost amounted to a pro-Israeli demonstration.

Pavel Kohout, a noted Czech playwright, drew a parallel between Israel, threatened by the Arabs in 1967, and Czechoslovakia, threatened by the Nazis in 1938. He justified Israel's striking the first blow because "a country as small as Israel cannot defend itself otherwise than offensively." The strong words indicated how much the Israeli victory had encouraged nationalist feelings among those who resented Soviet domination.

The discontent born of outraged national pride, economic dissatisfaction, and other factors exploded anew in 1968. For eight months Czechoslovakia offered the other peoples of

72

"Socialism with a Human Face"

Eastern Europe a vision of an attractive alternative to the Soviet model: "socialism with a human face," as Alexander Dubcek, leader of the liberalization in Prague, termed it. Poland was shaken that year by widespread student riots. Even relatively free Yugoslavia learned that Tito's relaxed doctrine did not satisfy the activist young, who conducted a series of protest strikes.

Dubcek, a Slovak, was virtually unknown to most people in Czechoslovakia early in 1968 when a revolt within the Czechoslovak Communist party leadership suddenly toppled Antonin Novotny from power. Still in his midforties when he was elected to replace Novotny as First Secretary in January 1968, Dubcek turned out to be a rather shy and soft-spoken man whose gentle personality contrasted sharply with that of most of the oldsters who directed Eastern European parties and governments. But he was the son of a founder of the Czechoslovak party; he had been educated in the Soviet Union and he had fought with the Communist underground during World War II. With such a strong personal and family record, Dubcek must have seemed ideal to Moscow. Yet within weeks of his elevation Czechoslovakia underwent a peaceful revolution such as had not been seen in a Communist country since 1956. The swift evolution toward genuine democracy apparently terrified the Soviet leaders.

The removal of Novotny, by vote of the party's Central Committee, was brought about by a coalition of dissatisfied forces: workers calling for better living standards, managers who despaired of getting meaningful economic reform, intellectuals demanding the end of repression and censorship, Slovaks infuriated by the betrayal of promises, young people angered by the police violence against the

73

Prague students who demonstrated in November 1967 for better housing.

After Dubcek took over, the apparatus of repression and censorship broke down. Neither the secret police nor the censors knew what was expected of them and the new leader did not hurry to inform them. Sensing the opportunity, journalists began telling the truth and speaking of the need for genuine democracy. They were encouraged by politicians—Gustav Husak prominent among them—who had themselves been unjustly imprisoned in the past, and by the head of the Writers Union, Eduard Goldstuecker. Dubcek finally broke the silence of his first weeks in power and spoke of the need for greater democratization, for making the Communist party the servant of the people, not its master, and for free speech and increased contacts with the rest of the world. But he always emphasized that Czechoslovakia intended to remain a loyal ally of the Soviet Union and a member of the Warsaw Pact.

In April 1968 the Communist party published a new action program entitled "The Czechoslovak Road to Socialism." A compromise document, reflecting battles between liberals and conservatives, it was, nevertheless, the most democratically oriented policy statement to be issued by a ruling Communist party allied with Moscow. Denouncing the mistakes and crimes committed under Novotny and his predecessor, Klement Gottwald, it deplored "suppression of democratic rights and freedom of the people, violation of laws, licentiousness and misuse of power." It also assailed management of the economy by "directives from the center," which had resulted in "slow increase of wages . . . stagnation of the living standard . . . the catastrophic state of housing

. . . the precarious state of the transport system, poor quality goods and public services."

All major groups support socialism, the program said, but socialism can flourish only "if scope is given for the assertion of the various interests of the people" so that "the unity of all workers will be brought about democratically." As for the party, the program criticized "monopolistic concentration of power in the hands of party bodies" and rejected the idea that it was a "universal 'caretaker' of society."

"Each member of the party and party bodies has not only the right but the duty to act according to his conscience," the program went on. "It is impermissible to restrict Communists in these rights, to create an atmosphere of distrust and suspicion of those who voice different opinions, to persecute the minority under any pretext—as has happened in the past. . . . People must have more opportunity to think for themselves and to express their opinions." Discussing the secret police, the document said: "The party declares clearly that this apparatus should not be directed and used to solve internal political questions and controversies in socialist society." The right of Czechoslovak citizens to travel abroad "must be precisely guaranteed by law."

Those and other ideas were so at variance with Soviet practice and official ideology that Soviet newspapers gave the document only cursory coverage, hiding many of its most important concepts from their readers.

A visitor to Prague a few weeks after Dubcek's election merely had to turn on a television program or read a newspaper to see that something strange was happening. All of the news media were suddenly talking plainly about the country's problems and telling the truth about Stalinist rule.

One television program explained in detail that Rudolf Slansky and Vladimir Clementis had been unjustly tried, convicted, and shot in 1952. The newspapers competed with one another in exposing the political scandals of the Novotny era—accusing Novotny's son of swindling the government in a complicated deal involving expensive imported cars, describing how the elder Novotny had forced the army to name an incompetent and almost uneducated crony to the rank of major general, telling in vivid detail about the drinking bouts and orgies conducted by Novotny's high-ranking associates.

A most moving experience occurred on March 10, 1968, at the Masaryk family grave in Lany, a village twenty-five miles from Prague, where Thomas Masaryk and his son, Jan, were buried. For almost twenty years the Communist regime had made a major effort to blacken the Masaryks' reputations and dismiss them as "bourgeois traitors." But on that cold, snowy Sunday thousands of Czechoslovak students marched to the cemetery to honor Jan Masaryk's memory on the twentieth anniversary of his death.

A bearded student climbed on a gravestone and said: "We stand at the grave of a man who died an unusual death twenty years ago, a great son of a great father. He was a cosmopolitan in the best sense of the word. He said in February 1948, 'I have always gone with the people and I shall always go with the people.' Let us remember this man at this crucial time, in which we hope people of the quality of Jan Masaryk will lead our nation."

As the deluge of unorthodox ideas advanced, leaders in Moscow became increasingly agitated. They met repeatedly with Dubcek and other Czechoslovak officials to demand that the reins be pulled tight again, that censorship be reinstituted, that new non-Communist political groups be smashed. Dubcek followed a policy that, in retrospect, seems startlingly like the tactic of that Czech folk hero, the Good Soldier Schweik, whose specialty was subtle sabotage. Dubcek assured the Soviet leaders that there was no danger of the counterrevolution or capitalist restoration they professed to foresee and he promised that the Czechoslovak Communist party would take measures to curb "excesses." But nothing changed—except that the volume of free speech and of political activism increased.

By June 1968 the Kremlin, now frantic, succeeded in forcing the Czechoslovak leaders to admit Soviet troops for what were said to be "routine maneuvers of the Warsaw Pact forces." The real mission was to intimidate the Czechoslovaks, but it was clumsy and it failed: the presence of unwanted foreign troops simply infuriated the people. Simultaneously with the maneuvers, pro-Soviet forces in Prague attempted to carry out Moscow's orders to clamp down on dissenters. Intellectuals, alarmed by developments, published a manifesto, "The Two Thousand Words," warning of the dangers of a return to dictatorship. There was an overwhelming public response.

The government in Prague then received what amounted to an ultimatum, delivered publicly by the Russians: Either Dubcek would muzzle the press and other media or Czechoslovakia would have to take the consequences. Dubcek, supported by the vast majority of his people, rejected the ultimatum.

A last peaceful attempt to bring the country to heel was then made: an unprecedented conference of almost all the top leaders of Czechoslovakia and the Soviet Union at Cierna, a small town near the Soviet border in Slovakia. In a wave of patriotism in anticipation of the conference, millions of Czechoslovaks signed petitions calling on their leaders to stand firm. A visitor found it difficult to believe that such animosity against the Russians could be mustered in a Communist nation.

After several days of tense confrontation early in August at the Cierna conference, which was attended by Brezhnev and Kosygin, Dubcek and his colleagues returned to Prague with the proclamation that they had won, that the Soviet leaders had dropped their demands and agreed to accept the Czechoslovak effort to make Communism more humane and more tolerable. There were reports that pressure had been put on the Soviet leaders by Western Communist parties and by Rumania and Yugoslavia, all backing the Dubcek leadership and all warning of the great damage that would be done to Communism if the Russians used force.

For a few days Czechoslovakia celebrated, though the news seemed too good to be true. It is clear in retrospect that Dubcek was not entirely candid, for he had made promises and concessions at Cierna about which he kept publicly silent. The situation remained essentially unaltered until the night of August 20, when hundreds of thousands of Soviet soldiers—along with Polish, East German, Hungarian, and Bulgarian forces—invaded and occupied Czechoslovakia and arrested almost all the members of the Prague leadership. Dubcek and his associates had time only to issue a statement condemning the invasion and calling on the people not to resist with arms.

The occupation was a marvel of planning and execution, but within twenty-four hours it became evident that Moscow had committed a major political blunder. Brezhnev and his colleagues had apparently assumed that a majority of Czechoslovaks opposed the Dubcek regime and that it would be easy for a pro-Soviet clique to form a new "workers' and peasants' revolutionary government" that would take power. Furthermore, the invasion aroused a storm of criticism, not only from the West but from many free world Communist parties and from Rumania, Yugoslavia, Communist China, and Albania.

Deeply angered, the people of Czechoslovakia united against the invaders. Students in Prague and Bratislava sought to resist by throwing rocks and gasoline bombs at Soviet tanks. Superior Soviet force made it easy to overcome this overt opposition.

What could not be overcome so easily was the passive resistance of the entire population, which was skillfully guided by a network of secret radio and television transmitters that, ironically enough, had been set up for emergency use in the event of invasion—from the West!

Signposts were torn down and local direction markers were turned the wrong way to confuse the invaders. Railroad workers sabotaged the movement of Soviet military trains. Signs and graffiti, many in Russian, denounced the invasion: "Ivan, go home. Natasha has sexual problems." "This is not Vietnam." "What do you say at home to your mother about our dead?" "The Russian National State Circus has arrived, complete with performing gorillas." People put up arrows pointing east and carrying the legend: "Moscow—1,500 kilometers." Most Czechoslovaks simply boycotted the invaders, but some young people who spoke Russian attempted to argue with Soviet soldiers. So complete was the opposition to the invasion that the handful of traitors who had planned to set up a pro-Soviet government dared not carry out their scheme.

The one major official still free, President Ludvik Svoboda, obdurately refusing to surrender, demanded that Czechoslovakia and the Soviet Union negotiate as equals and that all the arrested leaders be set free and recognized as lawful representatives. The Russians surrendered on the matter and flew Svoboda to Moscow. Meanwhile, Dubcek and his comrades, who had been treated brutally and insultingly after their arrest, were freed. The negotiations were unequal, of course. The Prague leaders were forced to approve the continued presence of Soviet troops and to accept a secret list of conditions obligating them to end the free press and other democratic reforms. But when Dubcek, Svoboda, and the rest returned to Prague, they were greeted as victorious heroes.

For eight months after the invasion the Czechoslovaks lived through a strange period—neither freedom nor slavery but a curious combination of both. On the one hand, their country was occupied by Soviet troops; on the other, the Dubcek group, still clinging to nominal power, sought desperately to maintain as much liberty as possible while yielding step by step to Soviet demands for repression and for purges.

Despite some restrictions, the press remained the most free in the Soviet bloc for a while. Time and again impressive demonstrations manifested the people's devotion to Dubcek and their continuing antagonism toward the Soviet Union. When Jan Palach, a Prague student, burned himself to death to protest the occupation, his funeral became a national day of mourning.

But the defiance could not go on indefinitely. Moscow used anti-Soviet demonstrations in Prague in April 1969 as a pretext for replacing Dubcek as party chief with Gustav Husak, also a Slovak and a politician who had originally supported the reform movement. Husak, terming himself a "realist," maintained that Czechoslovakia must bow to Soviet power, accept Moscow's demands, and accommodate itself to the consequences of its weakness. In practice, his rule meant reimposition of full satellite status. The remaining liberal figures were purged and replaced by men ready to obey Moscow's orders. Some months later Dubcek, after a brief spell as Czechoslovak envoy to Turkey, was expelled from the party and denounced. The press, radio, and television were also brought under strict control.

Czechoslovakia was tied tightly to the Soviet Union by a new "friendship" treaty. In effect it accepted the Soviet contention—usually termed the Brezhnev Doctrine—that Moscow had the right to intervene in any Communist state when Soviet leaders felt that Communist rule there was endangered. Even before the treaty, Husak and his collaborators agreed that the invasion had been an act of friendship. They ceremonially expunged from the record the official protest against the invasion, thus retroactively legalizing the occupation. But Husak managed to restrain the most pro-Soviet elements that wanted to put Dubcek and his associates on trial as "traitors" and "imperialist agents." By the early 1970's, Czechoslovakia was again totally subjugated.

Poland went through a complex evolution during 1968–1972, experiencing what were in effect two separate and isolated revolts. The first, in March 1968, was touched off by discontent and anti-Soviet feeling among Polish intellectuals and students; the second revolt, which exploded in December 1970 and continued in lower key during the first months of 1971, was sparked by working-class dissatisfaction and bitterness over the country's low standard of living. In 1968 Gomulka's regime disposed of the wave of student demonstrations with little difficulty. In 1970 the dissatisfied workers quickly ended Gomulka's fourteen-year reign as the boss of Poland. Let us look at these two dramatic episodes more closely.

The anti-Soviet resentment of Polish intellectuals and students had been simmering a long time before it reached a climax early in 1968. The revolt began when Gomulka ordered a Warsaw theater to stop showing a drama by the great nineteenth-century writer, Adam Mickiewicz, who described Poland's suffering under Russian oppression. Night after night audiences were turning the performances into demonstrations against Moscow by giving thunderous applause to such lines as: "Polish history is conducted in a prison cell." "We Poles have sold our souls to Moscow for silver rubles"; and "Everyone sent here from Moscow is either a jackass, a fool or a spy."

The closing precipitated major riots and demonstrations in March 1968 at every Polish university, during which students shouted slogans supporting Czechoslovakia and cried: "Poland awaits her Dubcek!" After the demonstrations had been put down—with extreme police brutality—the government and its supporters in Moscow looked for means to prevent the spread of active discontent to the working class.

Sensing an opportunity to displace Gomulka, Mieczyslaw Moczar, who as Minister of the Interior was head of the internal security forces, initiated a major anti-Semitic campaign. The student demonstrations, newspapers told their readers day after day, were really a Zionist plot to undermine Poland. Lists of arrested students were printed, along with the names of their parents. Most of the carefully selected parents publicized were Jews holding important government or academic posts. From Moczar's point of view, the campaign had the merit not only of appealing to a long anti-Semitic tradition but also of striking a covert blow at Gomulka, whose wife was of Jewish origin. There was no mention that Poland had only 25,000 Jews, most of them elderly pensioners, and that at most only a few hundred of the tens of thousands of demonstrating students were Jews.

Purges forced numerous Jews and dissenting non-Jewish intellectuals out of their jobs. As a climax, the Jews were accused of being loyal to Israel rather than to Poland and were told they could emigrate. Deprived of their jobs, surrounded by suspicion and hatred, thousands left the country. Among them were many Communists who had always been anti-Zionist, knew and cared nothing about Judaism, and nevertheless found themselves tarred as Jewish traitors so that they had no future in Poland.

The campaign's objective was achieved for the time being, and the discontent in Poland was contained long enough to make the Warsaw regime one of Moscow's firmest allies against Dubcek's Czechoslovakia. Moczar's hope of displacing Gomulka in 1968 failed to be realized, however, because Moscow viewed the secret police chief as an extreme nationalist who might cause trouble if he ruled Poland. A third

Polish leader who played a key role during those turbulent months was Edward Gierek, the Communist party chief of Silesia, who also coveted power and initially played a major role in the anti-Semitic campaign.

But the tranquillity won by these tactics lasted only two years, and in December 1970 Gomulka was blasted from power by an unexpected explosion of working-class political discontent. The immediate background to that crisis was the poor functioning of the Polish economy, particularly the serious setbacks suffered by Polish agriculture in 1969 and 1970. With grain and meat production inadequate to satisfy all Poland's needs, Gomulka decided to alter the pattern of his nation's consumption. His aim was to cut purchases of meat, clothing and other such scarce daily essentials by raising their prices, while increasing purchases of relatively abundant tape recorders, television sets, and other durable consumer goods by cutting the prices. But many Polish workers were outraged by these moves, especially since they were introduced without warning two weeks before Christmas.

The wave of anger among Poland's workers was general throughout the country, but it exploded into violent near-revolution in such Baltic coastal cities as Gdansk, Gdynia, and Szczecin. Soon there were many dead and wounded as the result of armed clashes between government forces and the workers, some of whom occupied their factories while others went on local general strikes. At first the protestors were denounced as "hooligans" and "anarchists" having nothing in common with honest workers. But as the protest movement spread it became plain that Poland was near the point of a bloody revolution such as Hungary had gone through in 1956.

To save the situation, Wladyslaw Gomulka and four of his top aides in the Polish Politburo were purged at the end of the stormy week of demonstrations. Edward Gierek replaced Gomulka as First Secretary of the party, i.e., as Communist party chief of Poland. Now the tables were turned, and it was Gomulka who became the culprit as he was accused of losing touch with the working class. In effect, Gierek admitted that the workers' anger was justified, and promised he would try to undo the damage as much as possible. And the new Gierek regime signaled that it intended to improve the strained relations with the Roman Catholic Church. One of the beneficiaries of Gomulka's fall and Gierek's rise was Moczar, who became a full member of the Polish Politburo during the political reshuffle of December 1970.

The mystery in all this dramatic chain of events was why Gomulka decided to raise prices—i.e., lower Polish workers' living standards—two weeks before Christmas. These moves would have been unpopular at any time, but they were sure to be most resented at that time. The great majority of Poles were devout Roman Catholics, and many of them must have viewed the price changes as a blow to their religious sentiments.

Gomulka's error in timing may have been the direct product of his greatest political success. The week before he had been the beneficiary of a visit to Warsaw by West German Chancellor Willy Brandt, who had come to the Polish capital to sign the treaty accepting the Oder-Neisse line as Poland's western border, thus fulfilling the dream of an entire generation of Poles. Gomulka may have calculated that the national joy at the victory over the Germans would sugarcoat the bitter pill of higher meat and other prices enough to make it acceptable. If this was his calculation, it was a disastrous blunder, and little more than a week after Brandt's visit to Warsaw—the high point of Gomulka's political career—Gomulka's fourteen-year reign was ended.

During his first months in power, Gierek found that it was not easy to end the discontent which had catapulted him into Gomulka's place. He began his reign with a series of concessions. He raised wages for the lowest-paid workers who had been affected most severely by the price increases and he promised to consult public opinion rather than rule dictatorially as Gomulka had done. But many workers, having got an inkling of their power, refused to be satisfied. The popular demand for a rollback of the price increases continued despite repeated assurances from Gierek and his associates that the country could not afford this step.

In the Baltic port cities, where discontent had originally exploded, strikes resumed as relatively well-paid workers demanded wage increases, making plain that they would not be content to accept the cut in their real earnings brought about by the price increases. Gierek himself was finally forced to go to the Baltic area to plead with the workers to end their strikes. But then a major strike of Lodz textile workers started, an event that made plain active discontent was spreading rather than quieting down. At this critical juncture, Gierek suddenly and dramatically announced that the prices raised by Gomulka would be returned to their former levels on March 1. Popular rumor in Poland attributed this policy reversal to a Soviet decision to free Poland from its 1971 "voluntary" contribution to North Vietnam and the Viet Cong. But diplomatic reports held that Moscow had stepped in and agreed to give Poland massive economic aid—estimated as high as $1 billion by some sources—to provide the additional meat and other goods needed to permit the price rollback. It was all an impressive demonstration of worker power and of Soviet alarm.

Gierek worked hard during 1971 and early 1972 to try to win popular support for his post-Gomulka regime, and also to consolidate his own personal power. He granted concessions not only to the urban workers, as discussed above, but also to the mass of individual peasants, intellectuals, and the Roman Catholic Church. Gierek's basic strategy was to ease or remove onerous restrictions that had aroused antiregime hostility during the Gomulka era. Thus the intellectuals were given somewhat more freedom to discuss important issues in the press, while some individual authors whose writings had earlier been banned were suddenly allowed to appear in print again. Some forms of bureaucratic harassment of the church were ended and its legal right to Catholic Church properties in the area that was formerly Eastern Germany was confirmed. By March 1972 Gierek felt sufficiently confident of popular support to hold a national election for members of the Polish parliament. The results generally supported this confidence, but there was enough dissent shown in the voting to indicate that not all Poles were fully satisfied. Simultaneously during this period, Gierek purged the upper ranks of the Communist party and the Polish government of Gomulka's closest colleagues. He also took care to downgrade General Moczar so that the once powerful figure might not challenge him as he had once challenged Gomulka. And when President Nixon arrived in Warsaw on May 31, 1972, Mr. Gierek saw to it that the President enjoyed a much more enthusiastic welcome than Mr. Nixon had received in Moscow.

A third country that had political difficulties from 1968 to 1972 was Yugoslavia.

In that country, long the most liberal Communist state in Eastern Europe, the gap between the commitment to greater freedom and the reality narrowed considerably in 1966. That was the year in which secret police chief Aleksandar Rankovic was removed. After his purge, it was disclosed that he had used his position to exercise extensive secret control over the country. He had named people to posts that were nominally elective, restricted freedom of speech and press, and even spied on President Tito. Moreover, Rankovic, a Serb, had presumably used his power to favor Serb interests. His political demise tended to strengthen those seeking full equality for all nationality groups.

The protest began in June 1968 with two days of bloody clashes between Belgrade University students and the police. There followed an eight-day sit-in at the university, a strike that won wide support among young people and intellectuals throughout the country. The students demanded greater democracy and more devotion to socialism among the people as a whole. On the first score they sought equal student representation on university governing bodies and more jobs for university graduates. In the wider sphere they denounced increasng disparities in living standards and wealth and signs of what they regarded as retreats toward capitalism. They also appealed for greater emphasis on social ownership and on workers' self-management, further democratization of the League of Communists, and freedom of public assembly.

Tito announced that he fully supported the students' demands and would see they were met. The promise was not kept, and in 1970 the students, still dissatisfied, were again striking, though with less impact than they had had in 1968.

### "Socialism with a Human Face"

Visiting Yugoslavia shortly before the 1968 student revolt, I was struck by the relative prosperity there compared either with the past or with other Eastern European countries. There were traffic jams, the shops had better and more diversified merchandise, much of it imported from Western Europe, and Yugoslav businessmen were proud of the rewards flowing from the profitable operation of their enterprises. Production had risen rapidly and the economy was also benefiting from the vast funds sent home by Yugoslavs who had been permitted to work in Western Europe.

Yugoslavia's internal divisions were temporarily healed for a time by the shock of the invasion of Czechoslovakia. That event stirred not only anger at the brutal treatment of a fellow Slav nation but also fear that Yugoslavia itself might soon be the victim of Soviet aggression. The government took emergency action to assure that the nation would be prepared to fight the same kind of guerrilla warfare against Soviet troops that had been fought against the Nazis. No invasion took place, and once more efforts were made to improve relations with Moscow, but tension and fear remained.

By 1970 Yugoslavia's foreign relations were sufficiently calm so that attention was again focused mainly on domestic problems. Tensions between nationalities rose and President Tito showed great anxiety about the possible breakup of Yugoslavia after his death. He set up groups to govern the League of Communists and the state in the hope that collective leadership would keep his country united. Economic difficulties also produced severe inflationary pressures, forcing the imposition of price controls and other austerity measures.

Tito's strategy in 1969–1970 apparently assumed that if

power in Yugoslavia were decentralized and more authority given to the various national republics and other local authorities, this would satisfy the demands of the nation's different peoples. But as so often happens, demands for greater local power increased even more rapidly than the pace of decentralization. In 1971 growing tensions among Yugoslavia's different nationalities became ever more evident, and by the end of the year there was a major political crisis in Croatia. Nominally the difficulty centered on a dispute over how much authority Croatian officials should have over the foreign exchange earned by the factories and other enterprises of this relatively advanced, industrial region. But soon demands were being heard for a separate Croation army and for other changes that came close to meaning the creation of a separate Croatian state independent of Yugoslavia. The Croatian discontent was made evident in a major student strike and in riots in the streets of Zagreb, the capital of Croatia. Tito moved promptly to end the danger. He purged the top leadership in Croatia, removing the key Communist and government leaders who had tolerated and to some extent even encouraged the separatists. By early 1972 the immediate crisis was over, but separatist sentiment still existed in Croatia and other Yugoslav republics. The result was that an even larger question mark about Yugoslavia's future—especially after Tito passes from the scene—was created in many minds, both in that country and abroad. When Tito celebrated his eightieth birthday in May 1972, he seemed more essential to Yugoslav unity than ever before.

Rumania's independent stance was made plain during the post-Khrushchev period by the arrival of two visitors: Chou En-lai in 1966 and Richard M. Nixon in 1969. Huge, friendly crowds greeted the Chinese Premier on a state visit at a time of extremely tense Soviet-Chinese relations. It was a bold sign to the world that the leaders in Bucharest intended to follow their own path. Despite the Vietnam war, the American President was greeted even more enthusiastically, showing Rumania's intention to be friends with all nations, not merely those of which Moscow approved.

The Rumanian policy was largely the work of Nicolae Ceausescu, the relatively young Communist leader who took over after the death of Gheorghe Gheorghiu-Dej in March 1965. Ceausescu not only welcomed Chou and Nixon to Bucharest; he also defied Moscow by recognizing West Germany and, as we have seen, by remaining neutral during the Middle East war in 1967.

The Rumanians under Ceausescu, like the Yugoslavs, felt shock and fear when Czechoslovakia was invaded. Since Rumania has a long border with the Soviet Union, the danger was even more acute. Washington considered the possibility of a Soviet invasion of Rumania so serious that President Lyndon Johnson issued a thinly veiled warning to Moscow. Rumania's reception of Richard Nixon the following summer was undoubtedly in part a gesture of thanks for that support.

Again the Rumanians were careful not to anger Moscow and to insist that they were loyal Communists and loyal members of the Warsaw Pact. The Russian's grudging acceptance of the Rumanian position was evident in July 1970, when a long-delayed Soviet-Rumanian pact was signed in Bucharest by Premier Kosygin; but Moscow's displeasure was reflected the weekend before the signing when Brezhnev, originally scheduled to head the Soviet delegation, canceled his visit on the pretext that he had a cold.

The Ceausescu era has been concerned with more than furtherance of independence. The party chief has moved to ease the Stalinist system, denouncing police frameups under Gheorghiu-Dej and rehabilitating their victims. Travel abroad has been made freer and the secret police have been curbed. Most important, Rumania has continued to move ahead economically, enjoying one of the most rapid rates of growth in industrial production in Eastern Europe. Still relatively poor, it has made progress by using Western technology and aid more boldly than most of its neighbors.

In the spring of 1971 Ceausescu incurred more Soviet displeasure by going on an official state visit to Peking, where he held cordial meetings with Chinese leaders and received promises of Chinese economic aid. There is some reason to believe that the Rumanian leader may have also acted as one of the intermediaries between President Nixon and Premier Chou En-lai in the period before Henry Kissinger's first visit to Peking in mid-1971. But when Ceausescu returned to Rumania, he instituted an ideological crackdown, demanding a tightening of the hold of Communist ideology on the Rumanian people. This and other actions suggested that Ceausescu feared Soviet action against Rumania and was following a policy designed to avoid giving Moscow any pretext to invade Rumania even while Rumania continued to follow an independent foreign policy. Alone among the Warsaw Pact nations in early 1972, Rumania praised President Nixon's visit to Peking at that time as a step strengthening the cause of peace.

In the late 1960's and early 1970's Hungary continued to develop along the lines Janos Kadar had laid down in the early 1960's. The basis of its foreign policy remains subservience to the Soviet Union. Many Hungarians, recalling their own subjugation in 1956, must have been extremely unhappy over their country's 1968 role in Czechoslovakia. But before, during, and after that invasion, Kadar showed his belief that the Hungarian government had to constantly prove its loyalty to Moscow if it wished to retain any room for maneuver on domestic policy.

Moscow has reciprocated by giving the Hungarians a good deal of latitude in their internal affairs, particularly in permitting major reform of the economy. Important changes were carried out to provide greater incentives and increased flexibility for managers with the aim of turning out products more competitive on foreign markets. Hungary was also permitted to develop economic relations with Western Europe and even to improve diplomatic relations with the United States, the goal being to attract capital and know-how from the West. More Hungarians were permitted to travel abroad and a major drive to attract foreign tourists was made, including agreements with foreign interests for the building of luxury hotels in Budapest.

It is a sign of the relaxed atmosphere in Hungary that such youthful dissidence as did appear took the form of Maoism among university students. The rebels felt that the relative de-emphasis of militant ideology and the priority given to raising living standards by increasing incentives were betrayals of Marxism-Leninism. On the other hand, older Hungarians, whose memories of repression and poor economic conditions were still vivid, were grateful; in effect they were willing to swallow Kadar's subservience to the Soviet Union so long as they could enjoy a tolerable life. The Soviet acceptance of this compromise, including even Hungary's relatively liberal economic system, which went further than the economic changes in Czechoslovakia that Moscow had condemned in 1968, was given public expression in November 1970, when the Soviet party leader, Brezhnev, attended the Communist party congress in Budapest and announced his approval of the Hungarian policy. But in early 1972 there appeared new signs of Soviet-Hungarian friction. Moscow appeared to be displeased by the extent of the Hungarian economic reforms, and to be exerting pressure by raising doubts about the future availability of Soviet raw materials needed by Hungary's economy.

Bulgaria, the Soviet satellite most devoted to agriculture, was also politically the most quiescent. It showed its loyalty by sending a token force for the invasion of Czechoslovakia. More important, it continued to accept the assigned role as the Florida and Southern California of the Soviet bloc, providing early fruits and vegetables for its allies. Unlike Rumania, it did not try to build up independent industries; instead its economy became increasingly integrated with Soviet industry, providing components for Soviet automobiles and computers. Bulgaria also sent thousands of workers to become lumberjacks in Soviet forests, where they helped produce timber for export to Bulgaria. Bulgaria also profited from the increasing popularity of its Black Sea coast beaches as summer resorts for tourists from the Soviet Union, East Germany, etc.

Until the invasion of Czechoslovakia the Albanian leaders were content with their political isolation. Using Chinese economic and technical aid, Albania, still the most backward country in Eastern Europe, tried to create new industries and to end the continuing hold of feudal customs. The ties with

China were so close that Enver Hoxha even ordered an Albanian variant of the Great Proletarian Cultural Revolution when the Chinese went through that phase of Maoism in the late 1960's.

The invasion radically altered the Albanians' perspective, raising the possibility that their country could be a target. While they voiced bitter protests against the rape of Czechoslovakia they also sought to end their political isolation. The press began to speak of the Yugoslavs and Rumanians as nations threatened, like Albania, by possible Soviet aggression. Simultaneously Albania began to try to improve relations with its capitalist neighbors, Greece and Italy. But when Mao Tse-tung and Chou En-lai received President Nixon in Peking in February 1972, the tone of the Albanian press suggested some unhappiness and some feeling that this was going too far in departing from the traditional anti-American line of both China and Albania. By mid-1972, however, Albanian-Yugoslav relations were more nearly normal than at any time since 1948.

# 6

# The Future of Eastern Europe

THE EMPHASIS in these pages has been on the efforts of the Eastern European peoples to achieve greater freedom and national independence since World War II. The yoke Stalin imposed after the war has been weakened, but in varying degrees.

Albania and Yugoslavia are genuinely sovereign states. Rumania enjoys considerable, though not complete, latitude, but it is linked with the Soviet Union in the Warsaw Pact and the Council for Mutual Economic Assistance as well as in extensive trade relations. Bulgaria, Hungary, and Poland follow Moscow rather slavishly in foreign policy, but Hungary and Poland have considerable independence in domestic policy. At the same time Hungary has undertaken the most radical economic reform of any Eastern European country, while in Poland agriculture is still uncollectivized, the Roman Catholic Church continues to play an important role, and Gierek has promised greater attention to the wishes of the people. The most fettered country in Eastern Europe is Czechoslovakia, still under intense pressure to eradicate the remnants of the 1968 liberalization movement. It is relevant, too, that Soviet occupation troops are in essentially permanent residence in Poland, Hungary, and Czechoslovakia.

For many Eastern Europeans, of course, the chief development of recent years had been their substantial progress in industrialization, standards of living, education, and medical care. In 1945 only Czechoslovakia could be really termed industrialized; in 1972 all were at least semi-industrialized.

If automobiles are still relatively rare, television, radios, refrigerators, and summer vacations are commonplace over most of the area. Housing is still discouragingly inadequate, reflecting the difficulty of keeping up with the needs of the millions who have flocked into urban areas. Medical care—often inferior but certainly much better than nothing—is widely available.

The new generation that has come to maturity since World War II is undoubtedly the best-educated in Eastern Europe's long history. That the education has been accompanied by intense political indoctrination does not negate its value. Moreover, the indoctrination has fallen far short of its goal of creating a "new man" devoted to the Soviet Union and its version of Marxism-Leninism.

Though economic progress has been made, Eastern Europe is still much poorer than Western Europe; on the other hand, it is far wealthier, on a per capita basis, than most of Asia, Africa, and Latin America. In the early 1970's average per capita annual gross national product in much of Western Europe and the United States was in the range of $2,000 to $4,000; the corresponding range in most of Eastern Europe was about $1,000 to $2,000, except for Albania which was at about $400.

The aspirations of the Eastern Europeans are, of course, the same as those of people anywhere: more freedom, more material prosperity, and more national independence (which means less subservience to the Soviet Union or no subservience at all)—in short, the opportunity to enjoy the benefits of the Western way of life, as exemplified by the hordes of Western tourists they see around them. Finally, and not least, they want peace and the protection of their national security against attack.

Unfortunately, most of the region's governments are in no position to determine their futures freely; in many areas Soviet policy is decisive. Let us attempt to penetrate Soviet thinking about the future of the region.

The parts of Eastern Europe the Russians dominate serve important functions for them—military, ideological, economic, scientific, and technological: the Eastern Europeans are a reservoir of military manpower to fight beside Soviet troops as well as a buffer between the Soviet Union and Western Europe. Communist control bolsters the Soviet effort to achieve Communism around the world. Eastern Europe is a major market for Soviet manufactures and raw materials as well as an important source of machinery, chemicals, and consumer goods. Trained Eastern European manpower assists the Russians in their competition with the West and Japan.

One may speculate, too, that in the long run the leaders in the Kremlin hope to "Russify" the Eastern Europeans and to incorporate them into the Soviet Union, as were the Baltic countries—Latvia, Estonia, and Lithuania—in 1940.

Moscow also sees dangers and disadvantages in its relationship with Eastern Europe. The Soviet leaders worry that heretical ideas in the region, which is more open to the West, may spread among the Russians. Fear that the Czechoslovaks' enthusiasm for greater democracy might prove contagious was a major motive for the 1968 invasion (earlier that year the Soviet leaders tightened their barriers against the spread of liberal ideas at home). The Kremlin is also concerned about the impact of Eastern European independence, limited as it is in most cases, on the minority peoples in the Soviet Union. If Rumanians or Poles or Hungarians are entitled to national states, why not Ukrainians or Uzbeks or Byelorussians? That question is never raised in the Soviet media, but it is such an obvious point that it must trouble the Soviet leaders, who are always concerned about separatist aspirations among non-Russian peoples.

The Soviet officials also see the possibility that they may get the short end of the stick in economic relations with the satellite states, although that may seem a remote possibility in view of Soviet strength. In fact, the Eastern Europeans maintain that they have been exploited by the Russians, pointing out that they have paid more for some commodities —oil is a key example—than do the Soviet Union's other customers. But from the Soviet point of view raw materials have been sold to the Eastern Europeans much too cheaply because they pay with machinery of inferior quality. Some Soviet economists have suggested that their government would profit more by selling raw materials in the world market for freely exchangeable currencies that could be used to buy first-class Western products. These economists have also maintained that the Soviet Union is losing money by selling raw materials to the Eastern Europeans at world prices because, according to their calculations, it is not recapturing full production costs. That consideration has led Moscow to put pressure on the bloc to invest Eastern European capital in the development of Soviet oil and mineral deposits.

The Brezhnev Doctrine is central to the Soviet policy on Eastern Europe now, with the exception, perhaps only temporary, of Yugoslavia and Albania. In effect the Soviet Union has put the world on notice that it is prepared to make any military or other moves required to keep the nations of the bloc within Moscow's orbit. The doctrine, not phrased so bluntly by Soviet sources, is usually stated in terms of the "duty" of Communist states to "help" other Communist states threatened by hostile forces. Since the invasion of Czechoslovakia is the prime example, the point is clear enough: Moscow does not intend to let any liberalization or change, gradual or sudden, alter its dominance. There are to be no more Yugoslavias or Albanias; even the future of Rumania is questionable as long as the doctrine stands.

Beyond that, the Soviet government is attempting to foster the military and economic integration of the Eastern European countries with the Soviet Union through the Warsaw Pact and the Council for Mutual Economic Assistance. There has been increasing emphasis on joint military maneuvers and standardization of equipment and tactical doctrine so that the Warsaw Pact forces could be directed as if they were components of a single army. In Comecon the Soviet Union has pressed for greater specialization and division of labor, increasingly close coordination of plans and the formation of more joint institutions. Significantly, the charter of the International Investment Bank, established in 1970, does not have the unanimity principle customary in Comecon institutions, so the veto power Rumania used in Comecon is not available. It is not surprising, therefore, that Rumania chose not to join the bank at first, though it did join later.

If the factors discussed were the only ones at work, a forecast of Eastern Europe's future would not be difficult. One would have to conclude that the Soviet satellites will become increasingly subservient while their economic growth continues. Such a prognosis would assume that Moscow, through pressure or force, will be able to compel Rumania, Yugoslavia, and Albania to fall fully into line. That possibility could become a reality; it cannot be easily dismissed in any discussion of Eastern Europe's future. On the other hand , it would be premature to accept increasing subordination to the Soviet Union as inevitable. At the least it is necessary to consider forces that tend toward alternative outcomes.

Eastern European nationalism is probably the most important of those forces. On every visit I have found abundant evidence that it persists despite a generation of Soviet domination. Rumanians boast that they have defeated Moscow's efforts to make them Slavs; many Hungarian young people are proud that, despite years of compulsory instruction, they still cannot understand Russian; Czechs and Slovaks look to the ideas of Masaryk for inspiration; Poles glory in the long history of resistance to Russia and there were anti-Soviet undertones in the Polish workers' revolt of December 1970.

If anything the events of 1968 in Czechoslovakia and Poland suggest that nationalism is even stronger among those born under Communist rule than it is among the older generation. Moscow has the military power to force its neighbors to accept absorption, but the Eastern European political resistance would be so enormous that it is difficult to believe that the Soviet leaders will soon be willing to incur it—to say nothing of the outraged reaction elsewhere.

While nationalism is the prime source of Eastern Europe's strength, it must be recognized that it is also a source of weakness as in the past, for it provides levers for Moscow to manipulate. Moscow can and does play off one Eastern European state against another.

In considering the outlook, account must be taken of the possibility of developments weakening the Soviet Union and reducing its ability to impose its will. A major conflict between the Soviet Union and China, for example, might make the Kremlin willing to pay a considerable price for voluntary Eastern European cooperation. To raise the possibility is not to predict it, of course.

There seems little likelihood that the United States will interfere with Soviet hegemony in Eastern Europe during the foreseeable future. It has moved a long way from the rhetoric of the 1952 presidential campaign, when there were hints that Dwight D. Eisenhower's election could lead to a Soviet "rollback" and the "liberation" of Eastern Europe. In recent years the United States' ability and willingness to intervene diplomatically or militarily have seemed at a particularly low point. Not only is it gripped by an increasing isolationism born of the inability to reach a satisfactory solution of the Vietnam war, but it has also been shaken by racial and generational conflicts. Simultaneously the Soviet Union has been rapidly achieving strategic nuclear parity, as measured by the power and availability of weapons, with the United States.

Many who had hoped for United States help to free or at

least improve conditions in Eastern Europe have watched evidences of American weakness and failure of nerve with disbelief and despair. But Moscow, at least, seems aware that the erosion of American power and will may be reversed and that the United States still has important assets in the world power struggle.

A new element entered all world political calculations—including calculations about Eastern Europe—with President Nixon's visit to Peking. As the Soviet press has made abundantly plain, Moscow fears the visit may have arranged a clandestine Chinese-American alliance against the Soviet Union. Whatever truth, if any, there may be to these Moscow fears, the Kremlin is undoubtedly more anxious than ever after the Nixon visit to assure the loyalty and dependence of its Eastern European satellites. To the Eastern Europeans the possibility may arise of using Soviet concern about the Peking-Washington relationship to gain further concessions. The Rumanians used Sino-Soviet tensions in the 1960's very skillfully, and the Yugoslavs—once regularly denounced by Peking—mended their relations with the Chinese and exchanged ambassadors with China as the 1970's began. It also seemed interesting in early 1972 that Chinese trade with Eastern Europe was increasing, while the wounds left by the violence of Peking's Great Proletarian Cultural Revolution were being healed. President Nixon's May 1972 visit to the Soviet Union may have discouraged many Eastern Europeans who saw it as implying Washington's acceptance of Soviet domination of that area. Senator J. William Fulbright's campaign to abolish Radio Free Europe also increased unease among independence-minded East Europeans.

No estimate of Eastern Europe's future can ignore the growing strength of Western Europe and its emergence as a major independent force in world affairs. The near-miraculous economic resurgence since World War II and the successful functioning of the European Common Market have enormously complicated Soviet efforts to keep Eastern Europe in thrall. After the Iron Curtain was pierced in the post-Stalin era, Eastern Europeans learned the previously hidden facts about their Western neighbors and wondered why they could not enjoy similar prosperity, freedom, and independence. Moscow, of course, sought to engender fear of Western Europe, speaking endlessly of it as a bastion of American imperialism and West German "revanchism" and trying to keep alive memories of the horrors of World War II.

Against that background, the West German-Soviet nonaggression treaty of August 1970, and the West German-Polish treaty of November 1970, are of vital import. The Germans paid heavily for the agreements, agreeing to recognize the Oder-Neisse line as Poland's western frontier and to accept the legal existence of East Germany. In return the Soviet Union agreed to more than merely a pledge that each side would abstain from using force against the other. It also conceded in effect that West Germany is a peaceful state that can have normal relations with all of Eastern Europe, a situation it had earlier sought to prevent. But in early 1972 Bonn's ratification of the West German-Soviet treaty remained in doubt. This was true despite East German and Soviet concessions with regard to West Berlin, concessions aimed at improving the lot of the West Berliners, particularly as regards their right to visit East Berlin and East Germany, a right newly exercised by many West Berliners at Easter

1972. But, finally, in May 1972 the West German parliament ratified both treaties.

Greatly increased Eastern European political and economic cooperation with West Germany and the rest of Western Europe would pose a counterforce to the pressure for increased dependence on and subordination to the Soviet Union. In East Germany, moreover, Erich Honecker—Walter Ulbricht's successor—fears that better relations between West Germany and the rest of Eastern Europe might weaken East Germany's position and eventually deprive it of the united support of the Communist-ruled nations.

There must have been bitter debates in the Kremlin before there was agreement to normalize relations with West Germany, but the Soviet leaders wanted to tap more of the West German economic and technical reservoir. No doubt Moscow hopes, too, that increased Soviet contacts with Western Europe in general will speed the breakup of NATO and bolster Communist and Soviet influence.

Normalization of West Germany's relations with Eastern Europe will inevitably raise the possibility of the reunification of Germany. There are few Europeans who will look forward to the prospect with pleasure. As long as the Soviet Union has a veto on East German foreign political moves, reunification is out of the question, but the day may come when the East Germans will break free of Soviet control and base their policy on German nationalism.

A modest optimism about the future of Eastern Europe has some rational basis. A quarter of a century after Stalin seized control of the area, its nations remain spiritually unconquered and politically indigestible. Despite the setback in

Czechoslovakia, they are far better off politically and economically than they were in the Stalin era.

It is worth recalling that the West has consistently tended to underestimate the opportunities of Eastern Europeans for independent action and their willingness to seize those opportunities. There will be more Titos, Nagys, Hoxhas, Gheorghiu-Dejs, and Dubceks in Eastern Europe. The situation breeds them automatically. It is characteristic of the potentialities in this area that the explosion of working-class anger in Poland in December 1970 was unexpected, particularly by the chief victim of the explosion, Polish Communist party leader, Wladyslaw Gomulka. For generations, moreover, the Eastern Europeans have seen conquerors come and go; it is not unlikely that the Russians will also return home one day.

The record suggests that it is unrealistic to expect the small, weak, and often mutually suspicious states to remain free of outside domination as long as each stands alone. A permanent solution of the region's problems can come only when its nations and peoples have federated. Nor need that federation be confined to Eastern Europe. The forces—economic, political, and military—making for unification suggest that some day there may be a United States of Europe, from Britain to the Russian border, that could bargain on equal terms with the United States and the Soviet Union.

# Bibliography

## GENERAL

Brown, J. F. *The New Eastern Europe.* New York: Praeger, 1966.
Dallin, Alexander, ed. *Diversity in International Communism: A Documentary Record, 1961–1963.* New York: Columbia University Press, 1963.
Djilas, Milovan. *The Unperfect Society: Beyond the New Class.* New York: Harcourt, Brace & World, 1969.
*Economic Developments in Countries of Eastern Europe.* Joint Economic Committee of Congress, Washington: Government Printing Office, 1970.
Griffith, W. E., ed. *Communism in Europe.* Cambridge: MIT Press, vol. I, 1964 and vol. II, 1966.
Ionescu, Ghita. *The Politics of the European Communist States.* New York: Praeger, 1967.
Johnson, Chalmers. *Change in Communist Systems.* Stanford, Calif.: Stanford University Press, 1970.
Kaser, Michael. *Comecon Integration Problems of the Planned Economies.* London and New York: Oxford University Press, 1965.
Kaser, Michael, and Zielinski, Janusz G. *Planning in East Europe.* London: The Bodley Head, 1970.
Lendvai, Paul. *Anti-Semitism Without Jews: Communist Eastern Europe.* New York: Doubleday, 1971.
——. *Eagles in Cobwebs: Nationalism and Communism in the Balkans.* New York: Doubleday, 1969.
London, Kurt, ed. *Eastern Europe in Transition.* Baltimore: Johns Hopkins Press, 1966.
Pounds, Norman J. G. *Eastern Europe.* Chicago: Aldine, 1969.

107

Seton-Watson, Hugh. *The East European Revolution.* New York: Praeger, 1961.

Shub, Anatole. *An Empire Loses Hope: The Return of Stalin's Ghost.* New York: Norton, 1970.

Sugar, Peter F., and Lederer, Ivo J. *Nationalism in Eastern Europe.* Seattle and London: University of Washington Press, 1969.

Wiles, P.J.D. *Communist International Economics.* New York: Praeger, 1968.

Wolff, Robert Lee. *The Balkans in Our Time.* Cambridge: Harvard University Press, 1956.


## CZECHOSLOVAKIA

Ello, Paul, ed. *Czechoslovakia's Blueprint for "Freedom."* Washington: Acropolis, 1968.

Schmidt, Dana Adams, *Anatomy of a Satellite.* Boston: Little, Brown, 1952.

Schwartz, Harry. *Prague's 200 Days: The Struggle for Democracy in Czechoslovakia,* New York: Praeger, 1969.

Szulc, Tad. *Czechoslovakia Since World War II.* New York: Viking, 1971.

Zartman, I. William, ed. *Czechoslovakia Intervention and Impact.* New York: New York University Press, 1970.


## HUNGARY

Aczel, Tamas, ed. *Ten Years After the Hungarian Revolution in the Perspective of History.* New York: Holt, Rinehart and Winston, 1966.

Nagy, Imre. *Imre Nagy on Communism in Defense of the New Course,* New York: Praeger, 1957.

Tökés, Rudolf L. *Bela Kun and the Hungarian Soviet Republic.* New York: Praeger, 1967.


## POLAND

Gibney, Frank. *Frozen Revolution: Poland, A Study in Communist Decay,* New York: Farrar, Straus and Cudahy, 1959.

Roos, Hans. *A History of Modern Poland.* New York: Knopf, 1966.

Sharp, Samuel L. *Poland: White Eagle on a Red Field*. Cambridge: Harvard University Press, 1953.

Woods, William. *Poland: Eagle in the East*. New York: Hill and Wang, 1968.


## RUMANIA

Fischer-Galati, Stephen. *The New Rumania: From People's Democracy to Socialist Republic*. Cambridge: MIT Press, 1967.

Floyd, David. *Rumania: Russia's Dissident Ally*. New York: Praeger, 1965.

Ionescu, Ghita. *Communism in Rumania, 1944–1962*. London and New York: Oxford University Press, 1964.

Roberts, Henry L. *Rumania: Political Problems of an Agrarian State*. New Haven: Yale University Press, 1951.


## YUGOSLAVIA

Campbell, John C. *Tito's Separate Road: America and Yugoslavia in World Politics*. New York: Harper & Row, 1967.

Dedijer, Vladimir. *The Battle Stalin Lost: Memories of Yugoslavia, 1948–1953*. New York: Viking, 1971.

Djilas, Milovan. *The New Class*. New York: Praeger, 1957.

Hoffman, George W. and Neal, Fred W. *Yugoslavia and the New Communism*. New York: Twentieth Century Fund, 1962.

# Index

# Index

general progress of, in Eastern Europe, 97; dependence of Soviet Union on Eastern European, 99–100
Education, advances in, 30, 97
Eisenhower, Dwight D., 38, 102
Electrical technology, Yugoslavian contribution to, 8
Emmanuel, King Victor, 16
Estonia, 98; and Hitler-Stalin pact, 17
European Common Market, 104

Foreign trade, nationalization of, under Stalin, 29
Four-power rule, collapse of, in Germany, 25
France: and Little Entente, 13–14; reluctance to stop Hitler, 15–16; and German invasion of Poland, 17–18; post-World War II, 21 ff.; and Tito, 35, 67
Free market, destruction of, under Stalin, 29
Fulbright, J. William, 103

Gdansk, Poland, 84
Gdynia, Poland, 84
German Democratic Republic, 25–26, 69 See also East Germany, Germany, West Germany
Germany, 9, 13, 14; and Great Depression, 12; invasions in Eastern Europe, 15–16, 17; post-World War II, 20 ff.; Poland's postwar fear of, 62–63; possibility of reunification, 105
Gero, Erno, 49, 52
Ghegs, 5
Gheorghiu-Dej, Gheorghe, 54, 56–57, 91, 92
Gierek, Edward, 84, 85, 86–87, 96
Gomulka, Wladyslaw, 35, 47–48, 58, 62, 70, 82–86, 87, 106
Gottwald, Klement, 28, 37, 54, 74
Great Britain: and ignorance of Eastern Europe, 4; reluctance to stop Nazis, 15; failure to appease Hitler, 16; and German invasion of Poland, 17–18; post-World War II, 21 ff.; and future of Poland, 23–24; support of Tito, 31, 35, 67

Great Depression, 12
Great Proletarian Cultural Revolution, 103 See also China; Maoism
Greece: U.S. and British dominance of, after World War II, 23; relations with Albania, 95
Gross national products, 97

Henlein, Konrad, 15
Herzegovina, 67
Hitler, Adolf, 4; takeover of Eastern Europe, 13–19; failure of appeasement, 16; plans to invade Soviet Union, 18–19
Hitler-Stalin Pact, 16–17
Honecker, Erich, 105
Horthy, Nicholas, 12
Housing, problems of, 30, 97
Hoxha, Enver, 36, 60–61, 95
Huns, invasion of, 6
Hungarian Revolutionary Worker-Peasant government, 52
Hungary, 4; national characteristics, 5; loss of Transylvania, 6–7; post-World War I, 10–13, 16; post-World War II, 21 ff.; predominance of Soviet Union in, 22; 1945 free election, 27; 1956 uprising, 38, 48–52, 53–55, 58, 60, 68; post-Stalin reform, 39–40; under Khrushchev, 61, 63–64, 92, 94; under Brezhnev and Kosygin, 71; and military occupation of Czechoslovakia, 78, 93; future of, and Eastern Europe, 96; nationalism, 101
Hus, Jan, 8
Husak, Gustav, 36, 74, 81

Immigration, Eastern European, to United States, 9
Industrialization, 7, 29–30, 97; in Rumania, 57, 92; in Bulgaria, 66
Intellectuals, revolt of, 44–45, 48, 55; in Czechoslovakia, 64, 77; in Poland, 72, 82 ff.
International Investment Bank, 100
Iron Curtain, 104
Israel, and Middle East war, 72
Italy, 6, 7, 13, 16, 18; relations with Albania, 95
Izvestia, 29

113

# INDEX

Jagiellonian Empire, 10
Jews, 11; as scapegoats for economic difficulties, 12; increased prestige in postwar years, 31; anti-Semitism campaign in Poland, 83
Jobbagy, Karoly, 44
Johnson, Lyndon, 91

Kadar, Janos, 36, 52, 63–64, 92
Kardelj, Edvard, 31
Kiev, 10
Kissinger, Henry, 92
Kohout, Pavel, 72
Korean War, 29
Kostov, Traicho, 35
Kosygin, Aleksei, 70; and Soviet invasion of Czechoslovakia, 78–79; and Rumania, 91
Khrushchev, Nikita: post-Stalin liberalization policy, 40–42, 45, 48 ff.; and Poland, 47, 61–63; and Hungary, 48 ff., 61, 63–64; and Rumania, 56–59, 61; and Czechoslovakia, 61, 64–65; and Bulgaria, 65–66; and Yugoslavia, 66–68; downfall, 70
Kumrovec, Yugoslavia, 3
Kun, Bela, 10, 48

Land reforms, 27, 30
Lany, Czechoslovakia, 76
Latin America, 97
Latvia, 98; and Hitler-Stalin pact, 17
League of Communists, 89
League of Yugoslav Communists, 34
Lithuania, 10, 98; and Hitler-Stalin pact, 17
Literature, as propaganda, 30 See also Intellectuals
Little Entente, 13
Lodz textile workers' strike, 86
London Poles, 23–24 See also Poland
Lublin government, 24

Macedonia, 5, 67
Malenkov, Georgi, 38–41
Maoism: and Hungarian students, 93; in Albania, 95
Mao Tse-tung, 59–60, 95; and support of 1956 Polish uprising, 47 See also China

Market socialism, 71
Marshall Plan, 22
Marxism-Leninism, 61, 93, 97
Masaryk, Jan, 26, 76
Masaryk, Thomas G., 12, 26, 76, 101; and creation of Czechoslovakia, 10
Medical services, increase of, 30, 97
Mickiewicz, Adam, 82
Middle East War, 71–72, 91
Mihailovich, Draja, 31
Mikoyan, Anastas, 49
Military occupation, unrestricted Soviet, and Warsaw Pact, 42 See also Warsaw Pact
Mindszenty, Joszef Cardinal, 50
Minority peoples: German, 13; Soviet, and Eastern European independence, 99 See also Nationalism
Moczar, Mieczyslaw, 83, 87
Mohorovicic Discontinuity, 8
Molotov, Vyacheslav, 16
Mongol invasion, of Eastern Europe, 6
Montenegro, 18
Montenegrins, 5
Muskie, Edmund, 9
Mussolini, 13; betrayal of Czechoslovakia, 15; invasion of Albania, 16

Nagy, Imre, 39–40, 63; and 1956 Hungarian revolt, 50–52
National characteristics, of Eastern Europe, 5
National Communism, 33, 41
Nationalism, 6; in Yugoslavia under Tito, 33, 67, 88, 90; Stalin's fear of increasing, 35; and 1956 uprisings, 46 ff.; and Middle East War, 72; Czech and Slovak, 101–2; German, 105
Nationalization of foreign trade, under Stalin, 29
National states, post-World War I formation of, 9–10
Nazi Party: in Czechoslovakia, 15; defeat of, 20 ff.
*New Class, The* (Djilas), 67
Nixon, Pat, 3
Nixon, Richard M., formal state visits to Eastern Europe, 3–4: to Warsaw, 87; to Rumania, 90–91; to Peking, 95, 103

114

ation to, 9; resistance to post-World War II Soviet imperialism, 9; post-World War II, 21 ff.; and future of Poland, 23–24, 62; support of Tito, 31, 32, 34–35, 67; inactivity in 1953–56 uprisings, 38; and diplomatic relations with Hungary, 93; and future of Eastern Europe, 102

Urbanization, 7 *See also* industrialization

Ustashi, 18

Uzbeks, 99

Versailles, treaty of, 10

Vietnam war, 91, 102

Voluntary cooperatives, in Yugoslavia, 66 *See also* Collectivization

Von Neumann, John, 8

Warsaw, 1944 uprising in, 23, 24

Warsaw conference, 42

Warsaw pact, 42, 51, 58, 63, 74, 77, 91, 92, 100

Wazyk, Adam, 43

West Berlin, 25–26

West Germany, 68–69, 104–5

West German-Polish treaty, 104

West German-Soviet nonaggression treaty, 104

Western Allies, and Eastern Europe, 21

Western Europe, growing strength of, and future of Eastern Europe, 104–6

Wigner, Eugene, 8

Wilson, Woodrow, and self-determination policy for Eastern Europe, 9, 10–18

Workers councils, formation of, in 1956 Hungary, 50

Workers uprisings, in Poland, 84–86

World War I, 4, 5, 6; and Eastern European immigrants in U.S., 9; and creation of national states, 10–11; economy and trade and, 12–13

World War II, 4, 5, 15; and Hitler's effort to conquer Eastern Europe, 15, 17–18

Xoxe, Koci, 36

Yalta Conference, 21

Yugoslav Communists, 34

Yugoslav Embassy, 51

Yugoslavia, 7, 49, 53, 60; Nixon visit to, 3; national characteristics, 5; post-World War I, 10 ff.; creation of, 10, 11; and Little Entente, 13; and Balkan pact, 13; German invasion of, 18; post-World War II, 21 ff.; 1948 Communist coup d'etat, 22; Soviet expulsion of Tito, 31–35; and Khrushchev, 41, 66–68; and Brezhnev and Kosygin, 70; 1968 student strikes, 73, 88–89; and Soviet occupation of Czechoslovakia, 79; 1968–72 uprisings, 88–90; and future of Eastern Europe, 96 ff., 100, 101; and Sino-Soviet tensions, 103

Yugoslav Macedonia, 7

Yugov, Anton, 66

Zagreb, Croatia, 31; student strikes in, 90

Zhivkov, Todor, 66

Zog, King, 12

082135